PAST A JOKE

by

ALAN ZEFFERTT

©1988 Alan Zeffertt

All rights reserved. No part of this publication may be reproduced, stored in a retrieval system, or transmitted in any form, or by any means, whether electronic, mechanical, photocopying, recording, or otherwise, without the prior permission of Portsmouth Publishing and Printing Ltd. except for brief passages in criticism or review.

Published and typeset by Portsmouth Publishing and Printing Ltd
The News Centre, Military Road, Hilsea
Portsmouth, Hants. PO2 9SX

Printed by Conifer Press, Fareham

Illustrations by Roger Purkis

Cover design by Russell Lewis

ISBN 1 871182 01 8

Foreword

I well remember being told that I would know when I was getting old because I would start prefacing my sentences with the words "When I was young....." At the time, I laughed and scornfully dismissed any such suggestion. No one, I insisted, would ever catch me using such a timeworn phrase. I had reckoned without the irresistible compulsion to reminisce.

With many people, it can be a dangerous habit: the saloon bar bore droning on about an illusory golden age, the politician reflecting on a time when life was so much more ordered.

Occasionally, though, in the right hands, it taps a seam of memory which is so rich that it is almost tangible. That was the effect Alan Zeffertt's manuscript had on me when I first read it. He had suggested that his "hopefully humorous memoir" might strike a chord in the minds of those who grew up in the post-war years. It struck a complete orchestral work as far as I was concerned.

Everything was there, from the first fearful day at primary school to the equally fearful attempt to find a job that would satisfy you, your pocket, your ambition and, if you were lucky, your employer. Then there were those strange and unpredictable creatures known as girls, who conspired to interrupt your progress at various critical stages of your life. And, of course, there was National Service........

Alan Zeffertt has skilfully cast his net over the past to give a picture of life which may be based on Portsmouth but could just as easily apply to Prestatyn or Perth, to Pontefract or Penzance. This is the country of childhood, adolesence and young adulthood, by turns funny, painful, confused and secure, but always observed with a sharp and original eye. Enjoy it as the guest of a natural guide.

Nigel Peake

A Memoir

FOR
MY WIFE, GILLIAN
TO WHOM
I OWE EVERYTHING

AUTHOR'S NOTE

This is my Portsmouth, seen through the distorting mirrors of memory and a sense of the ridiculous. Here are the favourite haunts, cinemas, theatres, dance halls and beloved Pompey football heroes. Recollections of schooldays and World War II jostle with the pain of National Service and the failure of numerous, ludicrous attempts at gainful employment.

Here, too, are close friends, passionately adored girls and the combined frustrations of being both teenager and jazz fanatic, when either condition was considered beyond the pale.

Most of the names are real but a few have been changed owing to loss of nerve and fear of reprisal.

This is how I remember the Forties and Fifties.

A.M.Z.
1988

Contents

Chapter 1 Early Daze 7

Chapter 2 Easy Living 9

Chapter 3 War Games 12

Chapter 4 Up School 17

Chapter 5 Set 'Em Alight 23

Chapter 6 The Way to the Stars 31

Chapter 7 Cosy Nostra 35

Chapter 8 Neck and Neck 42

Chapter 9 Shouldering Arms 50

Chapter 10 Junk Man 55

Chapter 11 Cool Cats and Hot Nights 60

Chapter 12 In Labour 65

Chapter 13 The Odd Couple 73

Chapter 14 Rose Rheum 78

Chapter 15 On the Floor 81

CHAPTER ONE

Early Daze

The rot set in early. I was only four but, with hindsight, I can see that the writing was already on the wall.

Sheila, who lived next door and was a mature five years of age, had invited me over the fence to share her see-saw. I had no sooner negotiated the wattle partition than she offered to show me what was inside her knickers. Panic-stricken, I scrambled back over the woodwork, shedding strips of skin and trouser en route and fled indoors in search of a less disturbing bag of marbles.

. . . . .slinking behind a tall, thin lady with a mouth like a razor slash.

And there you have the story of my life in microcosm. On the few occasions that I have been presented with a chance to glimpse the promised land, I have either looked in the wrong direction or shunned the opportunity altogether.

Then there was my urinary problem. It was a time everyone remembers – their first day at school. At 8.30 on a cold, windy morning in September, 1936, my mother and I stood apprehensively outside the railings of Lyndhurst Road Infants School, scanning the dozens of milling tots for a friendly face. The only one I recognised was Maurice Stevens, already a Bunter in embryo complete with sly Cheshire cat smile. I shouted his name, said goodbye to my anxious mother and ran into the playground.

Maurice had a compulsive need to stir up trouble from which he would expertly and swiftly extricate himself, leaving the blame and recriminations to others. For the moment, though, he was all I had. The chill weather and my fear of the unknown combined to produce an urgent need to pee. Maurice led me to a corrugated iron construction in one corner of the playground, explaining that he had been twice already but was willing to try for a hat-trick. We stood side by side in the primitive urinal. As I started to pee, it shot out at a 45-degree angle to the left – it did, sometimes – all down Maurice's knee-length grey socks and over his shining, new black shoes. He burst into tears at once, something he did rather often, and dashed, blubbing, into the school building to appear shortly afterwards, slinking behind a tall thin lady with a mouth like a razor slash. She brushed aside my protestations that nature had played a foul trick on me and, clamping an iron hand over my wrist, dragged me, still trying to explain my physical deformity, inside the school.

I received three strokes with the cane on each upturned palm and was threatened with greater violence if I failed to curb my perverted habit of urinating on people. Thus began my schooldays and, in retrospect, I suppose this tragic affair may best be considered a weighty parable. It imparts a powerful message: any relief from the pressures of life is merely temporary as the world speedily contrives to whack the hell out of you before you feel the benefit.

CHAPTER TWO

Easy Living

Portsmouth was never beautiful. It offers no challenge to Bath, Salisbury, York, anywhere. Much of it, endless rows of identical, tightly packed Victorian terracing, is cosily unprepossessing. After Hitler had removed great chunks of the city, the post-war breed of architects seized their opportunity and replaced that which had been merely undistinguished with vast grey blocks of appalling ugliness. Fortunately, the warmth, corporate spirit and generous nature of the inhabitants remains intact.

Southsea was, is, several social cuts above Portsmouth to which it cleaves, joined by an invisible seam. You cross Fratton Bridge and you're there. Gradually, the multitude of shops purvey a slightly better class of goods until they blossom into the up-market area of Palmerston and Osborne roads. Southsea has a faded Victorian gentility accentuated by the large, many-storeyed family homes, a plethora of guest houses and hotels and the lengthy, attractive, unspoiled sea-front. A stroll along the twisty, irregular, friendly streets invariably conjures up, for me, a kaleidoscope of pre-war memories.

I remember the Mikado Cafe, where my family gathered for tea every Wednesday. I sat at a balcony table, entranced by the turquoise decor, the fountain, the goldfish pool and the trio playing medleys of light classics. The music was even more to my taste at the Savoy ballroom, opposite the South Parade Pier. Taken by my parents, who loved the Sunday afternoon tea-dances, I rapidly learned all the currently popular songs and would hang around the bandstand, ignoring the leader's whispered exhortations to "Sod off, shrimp!" The band's gleaming instruments fascinated me and my lifelong love affair with music had begun.

Back home, I would arrange my toy animals into ranks like an orchestra. Spot, the dog (trumpet), and Teddy (saxophone) were the star instrumentalists while Coronation Jim, a three foot high doll and hoop-la prize from the fair at Clarence Pier, played bass. (Bass players are always huge.) Naturally, I was the bandleader, sang the vocals and improvised the solos with sounds that I thought approximated each featured instrument. We could have been a nationwide success but the boys in the band didn't want to travel.

Even today, the tinkling sound of a triangle instantly transports me to the aisle seats in row 5 of the stalls at the Kings Theatre, where my parents had a regular Wednesday evening booking. Plays, ballet, musicals were all magical, though I barely understood what was unfolding before me. I comprehended even less of the broad vulgarity of Max Miller and the lesser stand-up comics who graced the boards at the Hippodrome, a splendid variety theatre sadly destroyed in the blitz. I didn't care, for this was our Saturday treat. Glued to my seat with equal parts of excitement and toffee, I was similarly transfixed by the line of meaty chorus girls kicking out lustily a few yards away. My obsession with thighs endures to this day.

. . . . .the distant figure of Phyllis Dixey posing rigidly still in dim twilight. . . . .

Some of the shows were considered a little risque at the time, though the distant figure of Phyllis Dixey posing rigidly still in dim twilight at the furthermost rear of the stage sadly failed to raise the expected torrent of lust in my infant loins. My mother refused to concede that Miss Dixey was naked, insisting that she was "wearing a skin". I had never seen an undressed lady before but I was, nevertheless, dubious about my mother's assertion. It was difficult to be sure in the murk but it didn't look like a skin, especially around those little knobs in the front. They were definitely interesting but I would need to make certain of the layout in a good light before getting myself worked up into a lather about it.

I was eight when the final curtain fell on our good times. Despite their comfortable existence, my parents were not great travellers and holidays invariably consisted of a fortnight in the Isle of Wight. Once the daunting sea voyage from Portsmouth to Ryde had been negotiated, my mother suffering only moderately during the arduous thirty-five minute trip, we would settle into a family chalet at Sandown, Shanklin, Ventnor or, in August 1939, at Gurnard. Various combinations of grandparents, parents and children contrived to squeeze into a rickety wooden hut that resembled nothing more than an oversized dog kennel on stilts. From time to time, some of us took off around the island in my uncle's Morris car, with its running-board and a windscreen that opened outwards. We sang frequently, the tune for 1939 being "You Can't Have Everything." It was one of those Thirties ditties written for the benefit of the poor and unemployed, propounding the philosophy that so long as you had "a song in your heart, a penny in your pocket and someone in your arms to love," the world was your oyster. Especially if the sun shone, too.

It certainly shone that summer and the day we spent at Alum Bay was searingly hot.

Foolishly, I was stripped to the waist as I clambered over the rocks, scraping layers of variously coloured sands into empty glass tubes. By teatime I had become a giant Smith's crisp. I passed the remainder of the holiday locked into a sitting position, my skin so unbearably painful that the slightest movement caused the greatest discomfort. I was grateful, if mystified, when we packed up and returned home a couple of days early, on the first of September, and could only conclude that the gesture was in recognition of my pathetic condition. Eventually, the reality of September 3rd's cataclysmic events permeated even my self-absorbed cocoon. We were at war. We would be invaded. And we were Jews. And we would swiftly become one of Hitler's statistics.

CHAPTER THREE

War Games

The first months of the war were eerily peaceful but in July, 1940, the bombs started to fall in earnest and it was clear that Portsmouth had been selected for target practice. The carnage all around us, which included the total demolition of my grandmother's house in Middle Street, spurred my father out of his dilatory ways into decisive action. Several months later, to ensure our immediate safety, we vacated the danger zone and moved to the village of Denmead, some ten miles outside the city. As a consequence, when the Luftwaffe missed Portsmouth, the bombs dropped on Denmead. High explosive, incendiary, land mines, the lot.

In a further attempt to thwart the enemy, Dad rashly volunteered for the Home Guard, which was rather like Liberace signing for Manchester United. When I look back over my father's 83 years, he does seem to have been one of those protected species who lead a charmed life. Indeed, he made a marvellous start on day one by being born at a time that rendered him just too young to commit suicide for Field-Marshal Haig in World War I and just too old for call-up in World War II. After a kick-off like that he was surely in no danger with the Home Guard.

On the other hand having surreptitiously witnessed several archetypal "Dad's Army" exercises, training and manoeuvres, I became convinced of the distinct probability that my father would fall from heights or into depths and drop dead either from doubling with full pack through wildest Hampshire or at the mere sight of his unsheathed bayonet. Or maybe shoot himself. In the event, he came through his self-inflicted ordeal without a scratch, an alarm or a promotion and continued with the very necessary war work of manufacturing naval uniforms. Accordingly, he ran the daily gauntlet of bombs and bullets, travelling into Portsmouth on a No. 39 Southdown bus. He was so finicky about his food that my mother would follow, each lunchtime, boarding the bus with a plate of hot food wrapped tightly in a cheesecloth to retain the heat as long as possible. It must have been hell keeping the gravy quiet but winter, summer, air raid or not, she never missed a delivery.

After the Battle of Britain was over, the war became fun for kids. And I loved the countryside, exploring the woods and fields endlessly when I wasn't at school or playing football and cricket. I learned about sex by watching the animals on Bendall's farm. Mike Bendall was my closest friend and one of thirteen children. Just how the family kept expanding I could never understand for whenever I called, farmer Bendall would inevitably be ensconced in the outside lavatory. He had the disconcerting habit of leaving the door wide open so that he could read the newspaper which, when finished, he would tear into strips for use as a toilet roll. He seemed quite prepared to sit there for hours, conducting affairs with heavy authority and had an uncanny knack of knowing exactly what was happening at all parts of the farm, despite his protracted immobility.

My one problem was Ernie Waydey. He lived opposite me and was born to run a concentration camp. For six months he made life very difficult, greeting me with a venomous punch or Chinese burn whenever we met and threatening to give me "a right duffin' " if I didn't carry out his every wish. I ran his errands, did work in his garden that he had been detailed to do and generally performed all the demeaning tasks that he could devise. "I 'ate Jew-boys and gyppos," he would say cheerfully, closely echoing the party line in Berlin and, for the summer of 1942, he " 'ated" me. The worm eventually turned when a "duffin' " became preferable to the unthinkable. Ernie had confected what he called "The Antidote," by mixing the leavings from numerous sauce bottles, used tins and assorted sewage gathered from a local tip and blending it into a potent brew, heating the vile mess in an old paint can. He insisted that I drink this steaming horror and when pleading and tears were to no avail, I panicked and flung several wild punches, one of which was stopped by Ernie's right eye. He burst into tears, rushed into the woods at great speed and never talked to me again.

1944 was quite a year. The war was hotting up towards the big push and I reached puberty. Suddenly, from being overweight, I streamlined down to chunky and found myself with boundless energy and an odd, growing awareness of mysterious physical changes. The manifestations were hardly original and consisted of endless hours of football, tree climbing, bicycling and genial masturbation sessions with the boys in the woods. There was nothing to show for it but it felt good for a short while, until the guilt set in. And the fear of going blind, mad and to hell. We all vowed to stop doing it – and we did. For the rest of that day.

Suddenly, Denmead was annexed by the U.S.A. First came the painted markings on the roads indicating the allotted space between vehicles. Then followed countless lorries, tanks, gun-carriers in an unbroken line all the way to Portsmouth docks and stretching back into the country, how far we knew not. For a few months the G.I.s became our dearest friends. They slept in their trucks, in our garages, in garden sheds or in beds if we had them to spare. They visited for meals or a chat and generously supplied us with copious amounts of their rations. It's the chocolate Hershey Bars that linger in the memory! Always friendly, invariably garrulous, they grew strangely silent towards the end of May and, as June arrived, they all had their heads shaved and were gone. D-Day for them was B-Day for me. I was Barmitzvahed on June 6th, 1944. I was 13. A man.

As with Lyndhurst Road, my first day at Denmead Council School had been inauspicious. Before being allowed to occupy our desks the class was examined for head lice. We were then assaulted with a vile-tasting spoon which, when not being rammed down throats as an aid to uncovering some deadly virus, stood threateningly in a jar of pink liquid, considered sufficient to sterilise the object prior to its disappearance down another orifice. The final test was for scabies and I was sent home when several darkish looking spots were located between my fingers. My indignant mother hauled me off the doctor, who verified that the "spots" were merely freckles. But he had to put it in writing before I was allowed to rejoin the form. A humble beginning but things looked up as I began to shine in class and I ultimately gained a scholarship to Purbrook High School, the first pupil from Denmead to do so. The Headmaster was so delighted that he put up a plaque, registering this historic event.

A few years ago, I thought I would impress my wife with my one academic triumph and took her back to the old alma mater to show her the plaque. As we arrived at the foot of Ant Hill, I was horrified to see that the cosy old stone edifice had been demolished and reconstructed as the Denmead Community Centre. Without much hope but as a final desperate fling, I knocked at a door and asked the occupant if she knew whether the precious relic might have been transferred to some other prestigious educational establishment. She disappeared inside and I could hear her shrill voice explaining: "It's this bloke. He's lost his plaque."

After a short silence came the quavery response: "What's he want a mac for in this weather?"

The old lady reappeared at the door with a glum face, shaking her head. "It's not here, love," she said. "Have you tried the bins round the back?" I thanked her and left. Van Gogh wasn't appreciated until he was dead, either.

1944 was also the year of "The Match". Just across the road from School Lane, where I lived, was a large, flattish field that appeared to be common land and was used by us sprouting teenagers as a football and cricket pitch. Apart from Mike Bendall and his brother, Gordon, there were the James brothers, Roy and John, mystifyingly referred to as Pidge and Our Kid by all and sundry. Ken Bashford was a tough, wiry, taciturn lad

"Have you tried the bins round the back?"

14

who behaved as uncomprisingly on the soccer field as off it. Dick Cutler was our goalkeeper. Dick was given to long bouts of unprovoked and uncontrollable laughter interspersed with gargantuan sessions of eating. He would appear at the field carrying a large white loaf of bread, still hot from the baker's, which he swiftly and ruthlessly consumed while keeping goal. Despite his appetite, Dick remained weedy and gangling, probably due to the fact that he didn't hang on to his food for very long. At 4 p.m. he would refuse to play any more football until he'd had his tea, so I usually took him back home where he would alarm my mother with his insatiable desire for "more bread and jam, please" and "more cake, please." The continuing spasms of giggling allied to his proud boast that he was "the fastest eater in the world," invariably resulted in Dick bringing up the contents of his stomach on to our carpet, shortly after the larder had been laid waste. This, of course, only made him hungry again.

We grew dissatisfied with the primitive nature of our football pitch and decided to smarten up the ground. Mike and Gordon brought whitewash from the farm for marking out, I borrowed my father's lawn-mower and shears and we decimated several trees in a nearby copse to produce goalposts and corner flags. Our G.I. friends provided camouflage netting for goal nets and after a week or two, the area unmistakeably resembled a football field. We began to attract a few watchers for our five and six-a-side pick up games and one day were approached by three strange, shifty-looking men. One, who wore gumboots, grey flannels, a blue and white quartered soccer shirt and also carried a football, was obviously the leader. The other two stood a few paces behind him, shuffling uneasily and looking at the ground. The spokesman introduced himself as "Fred, from the big house, over there." He waved a vague arm towards the road. Fred was a beefy six-footer with black, greasy hair and a raw, red face. "We'd like to play your lot. Sort of a challenge match," he announced aggressively. We were delirious. A real game! We fixed a date and trained fiercely in preparation for the big day. The general consensus of opinion was that it would be a smart move if we all had a haircut, so we descended upon the local hairdresser, Mr. Button. He was certainly no Vidal Sassoon and his treatment of anyone under the age of 18 was always the same. The pudding basin was placed on the head and everything that lived below it was savagely destroyed with the clippers. Still, we all looked the same afterwards. Like a team from Borstal.

Our date with destiny duly arrived. The eleven positions in the team were filled, albeit with some difficulty; everyone wore a white shirt of sorts together with a varied collection of shorts and socks. Just before the three o'clock kick-off, Fred appeared at the corner of the field leading an odd, stumbling, shambling bunch of men. As they drew closer it became clear that there was something curious about them; indeed, we learned some time later that "the big house over there" was a mental institution. When you are a kid, however, such things are of little importance. Our opponents were simply eleven blokes from "over there." We watched as they slowly, very slowly, changed into blue and white quartered shirts, white shorts and blue socks. Very smart. They shuffled morosely into their positions and the match commenced.

As the game progressed, several members of our opposition manifested strange behaviour patterns. The tall, shaven-headed deathly pale right-half, appropriately named Chalky, lurked menacingly on his side of the field, gently frothing at the mouth. He swore violently and incessantly: "You bastards! You bloody bastards! Give us it, give us it, you bastards!" We tried to play on another part of the pitch but the inside-left was equally distracting. "He-he-he," he would cackle mirthlessly to himself. Fred, captain and caretaker, would scream at him after each outburst: "Shut up, Ron! Shut up!" But to no avail. Ron would look shifty for a few seconds then start chortling again.

Most magnetic of all was our opposing goalkeeper. A thin, bent over man of indeterminate age whom Fred addressed as Rattler, he was supremely active when play moved to the other end, away from him. He practised diving, leaping high into the top corners and low down by the posts, making fantastic imaginary one-handed saves. He was smothered in mud long before he was required to make a real save and this he affected, not with one of his swallow-like dives but by rushing out of his goal and wildly hacking the ball into touch. "Well done, Rattler," bellowed Fred. The keeper gave a secret, twisted smile and shuffled back between the posts. His luck ran out shortly afterwards. Bringing off another imaginary blinder up in the top left corner, he fell backwards and became entangled in the netting. His thrashing struggles to free himself pulled the net off the crossbar and in a few seconds he was writhing on the ground like a trapped boa-constrictor, entirely hidden within folds of camouflage. While so ensnared, Fred wheeled on his left foot at the edge of his own penalty area and passed the ball back to the goalie. The heaving mound continued its paroxysm by the left post as the ball rolled gently inside the right one. It was the only goal of the game.

Our reserve, David Addy, who had refereed the match as if he came from the big house himself, fled for home as he blew for full-time. Fred congratulated us grudgingly while his side trudged, muttering and cackling, back to where their clothes lay. The begrimed and lately released Rattler returned with what appeared to be a ball of newspaper. Fred unwrapped it and handed me a battered EPNS ashtray.

"The cup's yours," he said. "We'll play for it again, next year."

We never did. By then, we'd found out where they had come from, so vile prejudice and parental intervention prevented a re-match. We never saw any of them again except for Fred, whom I glimpsed sitting in the back of a Southdown bus, months later. He was still wearing the blue and white quartered football shirt. We kept the "cup."

Back at Purbrook High School all was not well. My usual first day trauma surfaced on cue and for this occasion assumed farcical dimensions. The pupils had been enjoined to support some commemorative football match between P.H.S. and another local school. In the event, it rained heavily and I found myself on the touchline with a few junior teachers and some doting females, all of whom were in love with the blond centre-forward. As kick-off time approached, our side were found to be one short and I was coerced into making up the eleven. Boots and kit were hurriedly found. The shorts clung to my generous thighs like sausage skins and bulged embarrassingly elsewhere, too. My delicate eight and a halfs were encased in boots size ten and eleven and a half respectively, both of them being for left feet. Being a right back by inclination and ability, I was moved immediately to the left wing where I played 90 minutes of inept and pain-wracked football. I limped off, saturated and miserable, to receive the coup-de-grace from the group of girls on the line. "Go back to Germany, Jew-boy," they hissed. I'd heard it all before and, depressed as I was, the wry thought struck me: why should they want to send me to Germany? I couldn't speak the language and I didn't know a soul there.

Classes were a problem, too. Purbrook High was co-educational and I was in love with at least 90 per cent. of the female half of the form. The abundance of thigh was driving me mad. I sat next to Eileen, a beautiful girl who had, unfortunately, contracted polio when very young, leaving one leg a little thinner than the other. She was, by far, the most desirable creature in the class and, in hot weather, sat at her desk with skirt hoisted to the hips. The view was sensational! I devised a dozen ways of dropping my pen, pencil, ruler or rubber on the floor just for a few seconds of heaven and another stolen glance.

There was no relief on Tuesdays, when I risked serious retribution and even grave injury climbing a tree that afforded a view of the senior girls in the gymnasium. On Mondays and Fridays there was gardening. Actually, there was two hours of groping, grabbing, scuffling and failing in the bushes. All I ever managed to grow in gardening lessons was another three or four inches. I was thankful for Wednesdays and Saturdays when I could work off my frustrations on the sports field but my work in class was dreadful and it was obvious that I would have to transfer to an all-male environment if I was going to pass the Schools Certificate examinations.

CHAPTER FOUR

Up School

By December, 1944, when it became apparent that victory in World War II was just a matter of time, my family returned to Portsmouth. We moved into a large semi-detached house in Kirby Road, very near the family business, but most of the fun was to be had in Montague Road just around the corner. There was Beryl with the pale face and teasing promises never fulfilled. There was Margaret with lovely long legs, violet eyes and pink cheeks which flared into crimson at the merest verbal or physical contact. Fortunately, there was also Marlene who wore glasses and kept changing her mind. We would stand in the darkness of the concrete air raid shelter at the end of Montague Road and start kissing. "Oh, yes! Oh, no! Kiss me. Stop it. Again, again. No – no more!" And that was just a kiss. It was exhausting, exciting and annoying at the same time. The slightest touch on any part of her anatomy produced extraordinary writhings and a flow of contradictions that left me utterly confused and willing to pack it all in for a bar of Nestle's Milk.

One afternoon, we were in the shelter and Marlene was going through her usual stop-go, yes-no routine when we heard a noise in the doorway. Standing there, staring thoughtfully at us, was a small elderly man in an overcoat and a flat check cap. We glared back at him as he peered intently in our direction through small, steel-rimmed spectacles. "I knew a fellow once," he said suddenly, "who flicked a digestive biscuit into some chap's eye and it ran out down his cheek like the yolk of an egg." He reached behind his ear and produced a stub of a cigarette which he lit with a match. After a few exploratory puffs, he wheeled about and stumped out of the shelter. Marlene and I followed shortly afterwards. There's nothing like egg yolk for damping down any post-prandial ardour.

The Montague Road VE-Day street party was followed swiftly by the VJ street party. Soon, the only reminder of war was the huge iron water tank full of stagnant green liquid at one end of Montague Road and the air-raid shelter at the other. Shortly, they would be gone and we Young Turks would have to find another place for establishing relationships and a makeshift supply depot for our water pistols. Portsmouth Grammar School reopened on January 23, 1945 – it had been transferred to the more congenial environs of Bournemouth for the duration – and the school's 950 boys and staff now had to cope with the forbidding grey building that had lately been used as a naval barracks. It was something of a shambles in those early post-war days, badly in need of repair, paint and equipment. Having duly passed the entrance examination, it was my first day there, too. The albatross remained about my neck for I was apprehended with several other intellectuals at the crucial moment of a peeing contest, when it looked as if I had every chance of reaching highest up the lavatory wall. The six whacks with a slipper were but an echo of the six on the hands nearly nine years previously – and the offence was nearly the same! It is best not to pursue this line of thought, I feel.

Despite Hitler's demise and the defeat of Nazism, anti-Semitism was alive and well and living in the Lower Fifth. I proceeded to use the classic defence mechanism and became the class comedian. It annoyed the teachers but it was a lot better than getting kicked in the balls every lunch hour. Gradually, the animosity faded, or rather it was transferred to another Jewish boy who was much weedier and had a less developed sense of humour. I sympathised but it's a tough world in the academic jungle. Being funny was time consuming, ultimately wearing and played hell with my grades. Physics, a subject I loathed, was made bearable only at 9.30 a.m. on Tuesdays. The laboratory faced across the High Street into houses and we overlooked a lavatory where the opaque glass window had been fixed the wrong way round. At 9.30 precisely, an attractive woman would sit down, read a newspaper and go through a number of familiar functions under the delighted gaze of the Lower Fifth. I always failed Physics. I failed at Chemistry, too. Indeed, I got off to a bad start when, fooling around in the lab, I mischievously applied the flame of a Bunsen burner to an experiment set up on the master's desk. There was a loud bang, generous amounts of smoke and a jagged hole in the ceiling that my father bought for £20.

Most of my triumphs at P.G.S. occurred on the soccer and cricket fields though there, too, I suffered the occasional disaster. It was during an inter-house football match that I placed an index finger against my right nostril and blew a gratifying quantity of mucus on to the pitch through the left one. Our referee, a rightly feared housemaster, Colonel Willis, stopped the game and screamed my name. As I approached him, the choleric cheeks, the gimlet eyes above the prissy moustache and the quivering indignation of the entire ensemble left me in no doubt that it was time for No. 2 to come in. "Never, never again let me see you propel effluvium from that vile orifice on to this hallowed turf." He sent me off and I was suspended for the following game as well.

The headmaster also found me less than lovable. In return, I considered him to be diffident and remote, much given to posing with his nose in the air so that he was forced to look down at you through suspiciously slitted eyes. I never received a kind or generous word from him and even on the occasion that I was made a prefect, he rose from his desk, pointed his chin at the ceiling and looking like a dolphin leaping to take the proffered fish, said frigidly: "I am conferring this honour upon you because I would rather have you as a friend than an enemy." Little did he know. I could not forgive him for replacing the school's winter sport, soccer, with rugby, especially as our 1st XI was such a strong and successful side, unbeaten in our final two seasons. One of our regular opponents was Bedales School, considered to be a liberal establishment where the students attended lessons only when they wanted to, called teachers by their first names and were frequently seen to be smoking quite openly. They were, sadly, a wet and weedy lot. Most of them appeared to be the privileged progeny of wealthy upper-class parents and played football in the same effete manner that they behaved off the field. Matches against them were no fun at all, for we invariably rattled up 15 or 16 goals and anything less than a dozen was deemed a failure. On one occasion, going for the ball in midfield, I was involved in a perfectly fair shoulder-to-shoulder charge with a Bedalian. He crashed to the ground and rose, eventually, crying pitifully with face and hair mud-caked but otherwise unscathed. The referee, a Bedales master, strode across wagging his finger at me. "We don't condone violence here," he said. I protested that what had happened was fair and within the rules but he shook his head repeatedly and looked sad.

"What hope is there for the world if behaviour such as yours becomes commonplace?"

I replied that my so-called offence couldn't hold a candle to what the world had lately been perpetrating for six years and this was more than our referee could bear. "I am grieved to do so," he announced solemnly, "but I fear I must take your name and report the matter to your headmaster."

Things were getting out of hand and I considered it wise to say nothing further to this idiot. As we trooped off at the final whistle after the regulation 16-0 victory, I consoled

Most of my triumphs at Portsmouth Grammar School occurred on the soccer and cricket fields. The author aged 16 (front row, left).

myself with the thought that, at least, Bedales always provided an excellent tea. I showered, changed and was making my way to the feast when the referee appeared at my side and beckoned me into the hallway.

"Do you enjoy violence, son?" he inquired, as my eyes longingly followed the rest of the side into the tearoom. I'd had enough.

"Yes!" I spat the word out viciously. "I love it." The master placed a hand on my shoulder.

"How are things at home?" He seemed genuinely concerned.

"Pretty grim," I muttered pitifully.

"Father knocks you about, does he?"

"Now and then." I tried to look brave.

"And your mother?" he asked quietly.

"On the game." I turned away as if wracked by the awfulness of my admission. He pulled a notebook out of a jacket pocket and tore off the top sheet.

"I shan't be sending in that report," he said.

"Thank you, Sir, thank you, thank you." I hoped that sincerity and gratitude shone from my eyes.

"Run along to tea now," said my Freudian friend.

I did so but the best cakes were gone and I had to fill up on the less inviting cheese and tomato sandwiches. The rest of the boys were in hysterics as I related my little encounter and we were still chortling on the way back to board our coach when the same master approached once again, beckoning me with his index finger to follow him. Around a corner of the building, out of sight of my friends, he produced a paper bag from behind his back and handed it to me, saying: "I hope this is the first of many good things in your life." I thanked him several times and dashed off to join the team in the coach. Once inside, I opened the bag and found three triangular cheese and tomato sandwiches and a fairy cake. It beats violence every time.

Every school carries its share of "characters" among the staff. The gruff, massive Beefy Pearce taught French with his cane – "my tickler" – in one hand and it was a crack on the palm for every mistake. Glaringly and malevolently owlish, "Pike" Parker was another eccentric, tripping over the doorstep every time he entered the classroom. Invariably, he would sit glowering at his table, wrinkle his nose and thunder: "This room smells of boy!" We sat, silent and guilty, unable to defend the charge. "I like you," he once told me. "You're a rebel, like me." Before I could commence preening he was in for the kill. "Unfortunately, I'm the rebel who is in charge here and as your work is disgraceful, you'll take a detention." I always forgave him.

Mr. Bartle, or Wally B as we all knew him, was my art master. I can neither draw nor paint. I have absolutely no facility or imagination with pencil or brush and am incapable of reproducing the simplest shapes, figures or objects. Wally B refused to accept that I was a hopeless case despite plentiful supporting evidence. In desperation, he told me that I would not be allowed to leave the room until I produced a reasonable piece of work. I hadn't the vaguest idea what to do but ultimately decided that anything was preferable to a blank sheet of paper. I ruled a one foot square on the sheet and sub-divided it into a lot of smaller squares. I then filled in each little square with a different colour and to give my masterpiece some character, squirted ink from my fountain pen on to the paper and rubbed it well in with my thumb. Wally B was ecstatic. "I knew you had it in you," he crooned, informing me that my abstract displayed a fertile imagination and the seeds of artistic ability. I consider it the mark of a true genius to quit while at the peak of creativity. I haven't painted anything since.

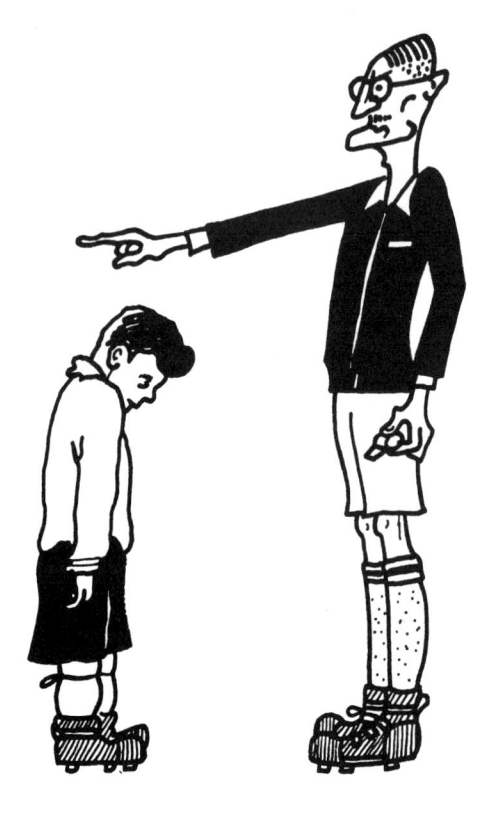

"Never, never again let me see you propel effluvium from that vile orifice."

The teacher I admired above all and to whom I gave all my attention and best efforts was Anthony Snelling. He taught English Literature and his dry, quirky humour, the smiling eyes set in a head that was always held slightly on one side and his utter approachableness induced me to read everything, anything that might gain his approval. Somehow, the chemistry between us was right, he understood, and beyond every other consideration, he was a marvellous communicator. I worked hard for him – and, thus, for myself – taking enormous pains over essays. I think back with deep gratitude to Anthony Snelling and can never repay him for the doors he opened in my mind.

While preparing for Higher Schools Certificate, I had on one occasion to write a critique of a musical work of art. Being a jazz enthusiast, I produced a passionate review of Duke Ellington's concert piece, "Black, Brown and Beige." "Splendid effort," nodded Mr. Snelling, "but you would fail in an examination because of the subject matter." I couldn't beleive that jazz would be so reviled and dismissed but I was soon to learn otherwise.

In 1948, the guest at the school's Speech Day was the famous conductor, Sir Adrian Boult. After his address, he asked the assembled throng if there were any questions. I rose and inquired of the distinguished knight what his views on jazz might be. "It should have been strangled at birth along with its protagonists and adherents," he sneered. The headmaster dutifully shook with laughter, a number of the staff smiled, some of the boys tittered. I was summoned to the headmaster's study later and admonished for insulting our visitor with trivia. It was as if I had brought the school into disrepute. My own reaction was equally ridiculous for I vowed, henceforth, never again to listen to classical music. (Indeed, it was not until my present wife gently showed me the error of my ways, some twenty years afterwards, that I relented and began to collect classical records. But jazz is still my first love. And I've never forgiven Sir Adrian Boult.)

Undaunted, I formed a jazz record club and arranged to give recitals after school, once a week. The initial meeting was well attended and even included a couple of teachers. I played some Louis Armstrong, Duke Ellington, Charlie Parker, Artie Shaw and Jazz at

In 1948, the guest at the school's Speech Day was the famous conductor, Sir Adrian Boult.

the Philharmonic 78s and was thoroughly pleased with my reception. Again, I was invited to see the headmaster. It transpired that he was concerned lest the parents of the boys who attended my jam session should object to their sons being exposed to such trash and, in any case, he did not want the school sullied by these alien sounds. I collected my portable gramophone and disbanded the club. I also found myself, as a suspected corrupting influence, banned from all music lessons. Well, I didn't mind that. I hated Handel's bloody "Messiah," anyway.

Curiously, it was while wandering alone around the building during "Messiah" rehearsals that I heard some beautiful jazz piano. I tracked it down to the main hall where I came upon 13-year-old Tony Day giving a trenchant workout on "Lady Bird," Tadd Dameron's eloquent bebop tune. A thin, pale and intense youth, Tony hovered over the keys in predatory fashion, brow furrowed, gaze transfixed by the keyboard. As the performance ended I clapped my hands in appreciation, causing the pianist to leap from the stool in alarm. After assuring him that he was not to be reported for abusing school property, he admitted that the sight of the instrument standing alone on the stage had been too much for him and he found himself impelled to give his first solo concert.

It seems that after formal training, Tony was bitten by the jazz bug and thus began a close friendship that exists to this day. Furthermore, we commenced writing popular songs together almost at once and in 1963 became a professional partnership. A considerable number of our ditties were recorded, some by famous artists such as Cleo Laine and Gerry and the Pacemakers. Glancing through some old books of my lyrics recently, I came across the first song that Tony and I wrote in tandem – it was called "You're Only Half In Love." It says much about the naievety of the times and of ourselves that the double-entendre in the title eluded us completely.

The Modern VI at Portsmouth Grammar School, 1948, with housemaster Mr. Charlesworth.

CHAPTER FIVE

Set 'Em Alight

Sometimes I feel that most of the stressful situations in my life were brought about by Portsmouth Football Club. I have gloried in their 1939 Cup Final triumph against Wolves, their magnificent championship side that topped Division I in the 1948-49 and 1949-50 seasons, and a thousand assorted victories over the years. I have suffered grievously at their several relegations and subsequent failure to return to the higher echelon. At the start of every season I tell my wife that "I don't care any more," that "it doesn't hurt like it used to," but it does. It bloody does. I have tried every possible alchemy to produce a good result on Saturdays. When I lived some 90 miles from Fratton Park, I was forced to practise my wizardry on the radio or TV. Thus, I didn't listen to the half-time scores/I did listen to them. I watched the results come through on the teleprinter – but only on the B.B.C. I stood up as the scores were announced/I sat in a special chair at 4.40 p.m. precisely. It made no difference – Pompey continued to lose the crucial games.

And yet, the love affair goes on. Wherever I live, whatever I'm doing, the final score can produce a whoop of delight or plunge me into despair. Only temporarily, of course, and nowadays I'm usually over the worst effects of a Portsmouth drubbing in about 48 hours.

But the good memories linger. Of the pre-war players, cheeky Cliff Parker springs instantly to mind. His behaviour would never be tolerated today but that is why the present game is so lacking in characters. When the action was taking place elsewhere, left-winger Cliff could frequently be found chatting to the crowd, accepting chewing gum or a drink or engaged in earnest conversation with his opposing full-back, whom he would appear to infuriate with incessant nattering and clowning. It was unwise to underrate him, however, for he was a more than capable footballer whose jinking and swerving sent many a defender the wrong way. His centres were wickedly accurate and he scored many vital goals, including a couple in the famous 4-1 Cup Final victory.

Tommy Rowe was a huge and massively effective centre-half in a long tradition of Pompey stoppers, totally reliable and almost unbeatable in the air. The tough, canny captain was Jimmy Guthrie, who later became an equally shrewd chairman of the Professional Footballers' Union, and I can still recall the bobbing, weaving dribbling of the bald-headed right-winger, Freddy Worrall. He was hard to dispossess and his low centres into the goalmouth were a constant menace to the opposition. I cherish the memory of burly Guy Wharton, plundering the ball and laying it on for Parker to go ambling down the touchline, a big grin all over his face. And there was centre-forward Jock Anderson conjuring goals out of nothing; classy Irish international Jimmy McAlinden, who kept the forward line functioning smoothly; young, ebullient Bert

Barlow, always surging forward with menace and shooting explosively.

During World War II, Pompey played in the London War League and I clearly remember an incredible match against Clapton Orient. After Bill Rochford had put through his own goal, Portsmouth went berserk, winning 16-1. Ted Drake, stationed locally with the R.A.F., scored eight. I listened to the football results that evening just to make sure that it wasn't all a dream and was amazed to hear that Blackpool had run up fifteen goals on the same afternoon, thereby stealing a little of the Blues' thunder.

But it was the post-war team that truly warmed the heart. By Christmas, 1946, Pompey were bottom of Division I and then came the turning point. In the final flourish of his career, manager Jack Tinn put together a potent blend of talent, character and originality that fused into one of those glorious sides that seem to have it all. He bequeathed this curious group of unlikely winners to Bob Jackson, who immediately steered Portsmouth to two championships in 1948-49 and 1949-50. The crowds were incredible – 40,000 was commonplace – and even the reserves regularly drew a 10,000 gate. The record was 51,385 for a 6th round F.A. Cup game against Derby County on February 26, 1949. It was frightening and exhilarating. Standing behind one goal, so tightly packed that I couldn't raise either arm, every lurch forward to view the action was a communal movement that involved thousands of people. Fainting women and children were passed down over the heads of the massed onlookers to waiting ambulance men but the discomfort and claustrophobic conditions were forgotten as Ike Clarke spun round on the proverbial sixpence and placed the ball low inside the far corner of the net for the only goal – Pompey's winner. There was a huge mutual ecstasy, encapsulated in the stentorian cri-de-coeur of that omnipresent supporter at the Fratton end, whose unvarying call to battle welled out above the chanted Pompey Chimes and the noisy hum of the assembled throng: "C'mon the Blues. SET 'EM A-L-I-G-H-T!"

After several euphoric seasons the road led inexorably downward to the ignominy of relegation in 1959. Great players left or grew old and were replaced by mere mortals. Management lacked flair and it seemed that there had been no consolidation or building for the future while the club had been at the top. It was as if the roots were already rotting as the tree was blooming. To this day, Portsmouth are still searching for the magic formula but, happily, I can clearly recall that unique bunch of idiosyncratic footballers who swept aside the other great teams for a few magic seasons.

Perhaps the only weakness was goalkeeper Ernie Butler, as likely to make an amazing save as to let in a soft goal. Fortunately, he was well protected. Phil Rookes was a cultured, intelligent and cool right-back, partnered on his left by the robust and forceful Harry Ferrier, one of the first full-backs, as I remember, to perfect the overlap down the wing. His clearances were prodigious, his tackling fierce. Even fiercer, indeed positively terrifying, was the tackling of right-half Jimmy Scoular. A bandy-legged, belligerent gnome, discovered while in the Navy, he took absolutely no prisoners at Fratton Park; but far from being merely a destroyer, he had the ability to break up an attack and create opportunities for his forwards with shrewd passes or unstoppable surges into enemy territory. This inelegant, spidery, awesome man was beautifully balanced by the studied, immaculate, perceptive play of left-half Jimmy Dickinson. One of the greatest players I have seen, Jim epitomised all that is good in football. A master of the penetrating long pass, he read the game several moves ahead of his opponents. He was an incisive tackler and I never saw him foul deliberately. He orchestrated play from the engine-room of the side with a fathomless collection of deft flicks, pushes, passes, tackles and dribbles. He deserved every one of his 49 England caps and it is a salutary thought that throughout a long career, every one of his 764 appearances was for the same club. At the heart of the defence was the trusty Reg Flewin. Reg looked physically out of proportion, his large head topping an elastic neck, a long, broad body but short, stubby legs. Time and again, that crinkly hair and florid face would rise above the pack to head away yet another

. . . . .a potent blend of talent, character and originality that fused into one of those glorious sides that seem to have it all. . . . .

dangerous centre and the elongated torso somehow contrived to block everything that threatened to pass it.

The forward line was an extraordinary collection of talents. On the left wing was the mercurial Jack Froggatt. Blond, chunky, explosive, he functioned anywhere and played at centre-forward, centre-half too, if required. Though of average height, he jumped higher than most, headed or shot for goal at the slightest opportunity and was a desperately difficult handful for any defender to contain as he bludgeoned his way down the left flank. Inside him was the conjuror, Len Phillips, who had never played soccer at all until he joined in a kick-about while serving with the Royal Marines. He was then already 19 years of age. He possessed an entirely untutored ability to dribble with the ball in the tightest of spaces and to avoid innumerable tackles with his natural body swerve and amazing control. By drawing several players to him, he could release the ball into the opening thus created, providing pin-point chances of scoring for his team-mates. Len didn't score very often, himself, and he was frequently castigated by the crowd for holding the ball overlong and occasionally losing it. Nevertheless, footballers of his stature are rare – today, they are like gold-dust – and the brilliance of his freakish wizardry will dwell forever in my mind's eye.

The centre-forward wasn't a typical big, barnstorming battler of that time but the intelligent, subtle, long-headed Ike Clarke. Operating in his own well-oiled groove, he set up chances for all the forwards while taking many for himself with beautifully placed shots and headers. He was the linchpin of a unique attack, his sharp nods and flicks timed to perfection – hallmarks of a true professional.

If my fondest memories concern the right wing pair, it is because this duo functioned so perfectly together and gave so much pleasure to the fans, despite their apparent incongruity. The first time I saw Duggie Reid, he inspired laughter and disbelief rather than confidence. Shrewd Jack Tinn had signed the Scottish inside-right from lowly Stockport County, where he was virtually unknown and already nearing thirty. Well over six feet tall, raw-boned, craggy and seemingly built of granite, he spent most of his first match falling over. He was slow, ungainly and appeared to be playing with his boots on the wrong feet. But he learned to stand up and though he never was a player of pace, displayed other, more valuable attributes. His shooting was deadly, not merely close in but from 25, 30, 40 yards. And the power in that mighty right boot was awesome. Goals crashed in from all angles; when he took a penalty it was a frightening experience for the keeper. I have seen him actually burst the net from the spot and, on another occasion when the goalkeeper got his body behind a dead straight penalty, the sheer force of the kick carried the keeper, still clutching the ball, into the back of the net.

.....the sheer force of the kick carried the keeper, still clutching the ball, into the back of the net.

Reid was equally accurate with his head. The ball simply flew from that red, rock-like forehead and I remember him scoring a hat-trick of headers, against Sam Bartram no less, one of them from the edge of the penalty area. Despite his size, forbidding appearance and never-changing expression of grim concentration, Duggie – Thunder-boots, as the popular press dubbed him – was the archetypal gentle giant. Because of his lethal shooting, he was mercilessly hacked, mauled and tripped throughout his career but I never saw him lose his temper or retaliate. He would pick himself up off the pitch, slowly and deliberately wipe off the mud, straighten up his socks and stride away with resigned, world-weary fatalism to take the free kick. And a Duggie Reid free kick was always a special event. The expectation in the crowd was tangible, the prospect of the explosion to come rivalling the actual blast of the shot itself in shock and entertainment value.

As if this were not enough, Reid was a master of the long accurate pass, above all the through ball inside the full-back that set winger Peter Harris in motion. Harris was, quite simply, the fastest footballer I have ever seen over 60 or 70 yards. If he received the ball in his own half he would glide past defenders, either down the wing or by cutting inside, in either event at such a speed that he was rarely, if ever, caught. His finishing was clinical, whether placing the ball wide of the advancing keeper or pulling it back into the path of an oncoming teammate. Nothing raised the supporters to greater heights of ecstasy than Duggie's long pass beyond the defence and down the wing, for they knew that Peter would be away at that precise moment, tearing past the opposition to latch on to the ball and bear in on the goal. It was a joy to have witnessed Peter Harris at his optimum. Duggie Reid went into the ice-cream business and later became the grounds-man at Fratton Park. He gave me enormous pleasure and I doubt if his like will appear again. His ball control was imperfect, he was occasionally slow off the mark and sometimes sluggish in motion. It wouldn't do today with all that 100 per cent. commitment, hair-trigger fitness and supression of individuality – but I know what sort of football I'd prefer to watch.

Postscript

The foregoing was written before returning to Portsmouth. The agony, of course, continued as, for a third consecutive season, Pompey flirted with the possibility of promotion to Division I, seemingly to reject the notion yet again at the eleventh hour. The anguish was such that I couldn't bear to attend Fratton Park matches, preferring to court insanity by switching on local radio for quarter-hour updates of the score. It was probably worse than suffering in person.

When, almost by default, Portsmouth were promoted – other challengers having fallen short – I felt that I could afford to luxuriate with equanimity at the last home match of the season, against Sheffield United. The result no longer being crucial, I would wallow in the atmosphere of success and jubilation, join the acclamation and triumph. I could hardly wait for the day, the hour. I should have been prepared for reality to fall short of expectation but not by such a margin. The portents were ominous as I threaded my way to Fratton Park a generous hour-and-a-half before kick-off. Outside countless pubs, groups of young men and younger youths were already legless, the beer cans littering the pavements, their belligerent chanting filling the streets. As thousands queued to enter the ground, the obscene songs rang loud and clear.

I sat in the North Stand, still hoping for a magical afternoon and the pre-match entertaiments augered well. Apart from isolated clashes with police, the 30,000 crowd was generally good-humoured and with Pompey receiving a tumultuous welcome, the cheering, the singing and a 1-0 half-time lead spread a glow of contentment around the ground. The euphoria swiftly dissipated as Pompey fell behind, 2-1. Their football, at no time better than ordinary – a circumstance I was prepared to forgive owing to the headiness of the occasion and the release of long endured tensions – deteriorated to the abysmal. It became clear that the home team were in no condition to save the match but then the celebration was also destroyed by hundreds of mindless youths who persistently invaded the pitch, rushing once with frightening ferocity and upraised fists to the corner were a few hundred Sheffield fans were mercifully penned in safety. The referee and the chairman begged the crowd to behave and not break down the fences as they would be allowed on the pitch at the end, to salute their heroes. The fences were torn down, regardless, as the hundreds on the turf multiplied.

I reminded myself that football was no longer merely a game. It was a weekly war between the young of two cities and the soccer pitch was the battlefield. The Sheffield goalkeeper appeared to foul a Pompey player once the debacle had restarted, but the penalty wasn't given. The venom of the crowd's response was chilling. I sat, surrounded by perfectly respectable people, parents with young children, many elderly supporters. A woman rose behind me and screeched at the keeper: "You bastard, you deserve to die for that!" Next to me, a small boy, no more than ten years of age, leapt to his feet. "Put the sod in hospital," he screamed. His father, well-spoken and obviously intelligent, said nothing in reproof. Around me, fists were raised, faces contorted with hate. The cancer was obviously worse than I had expected.

The pitch invasions continued. Further appeals proved fruitless as twenty minutes passed and thousands gathered on the field of play. I couldn't take any more. As I left I noted a number of glum faces and shaking heads in the crowd. The silent majority, I dared to hope. Outside the ground, a steward was relating how a drunken youngster had thrust a broken bottle into his face, demanding free admission. Policemen with dogs stood gloomily next to their barred wagons, waiting for the onslaught and chaos after the final whistle.

I listened to the match reports on radio, read the local papers and followed the hours of triumphal rejoicing at the Guildhall, broadcast the day after. Certainly, there was no condemnation of the disgraceful exhibtion which, sadly, received scant attention from the media. Rather, it was excusable, the fans had waited so long for success. Their disappointments and frustrations had built up. It was a time to forgive and forget.

Perhaps I'm getting old and out of touch. It had been some while since I last attended a football match – maybe, this moronic behaviour was so commonplace that it was now condoned and accepted. I believe that Pompey simply had to get promotion this season and they didn't much care how it was achieved. They didn't care about the manner of the team's performances as long as the final results were satisfactory. Skill was sacrificed for the ends that would justify the means. I consider that this same heartless, uncaring attitude was transmitted to many young supporters, who reflected it in their own conduct.

On their long journey back to Division I, Portsmouth lost much more than football matches. They lost sight of the fact that soccer is still a game required to give pleasure to players and supporters alike. Not merely pleasure in victory but in the manner of its achievement. And if not a victory, then pleasure in the skills, the performance, the endeavour.

Today, of course, it is a crime to be a loser – because of the money and the shame, but mainly because of the money. The big money goes to the winners and players want to play for clubs that win. They pay more. Most supporters will only follow a winning team, for a losing side projects an aura of failure into their lives, making them feel inferior. For some young fans, a successful football team is the only thing of promise in a hard,

The trusty Reg Flewin. Time and again that crinkly hair and florid face would rise above the pack.

Jimmy Dickinson epitomised all that is good in football

unpromising world. It offers a reflected glory, contains glamour and excitement. If the team fails, their only remaining route to media attention and a kind of notoriety is through violence and attrition.

Well, here I make no apology for being old-fashioned. I've supported Pompey all my life because I was born in the city and it was the natural, loyal thing to do, no matter how their fortunes fluctuated. But I can't go back to Fratton Park until and unless attitudes change, both on and off the pitch. I don't need to spend more money than I can cheerfully afford watching society's ills paraded before me in a 90-minute microcosm. Oh, I'll still be listening for the results every match day and my heart will be beating a little faster around 4.40 p.m. each Saturday. And there'll be a brief flicker of pleasure or moment of sadness, depending upon the result. But the lifelong passion and obsession was shattered during that match with Sheffield United. That broken bottle, as it were, finally severed the umbilical cord.

I'm glad Pompey were promoted, though I feel only a muted pride in the achievement. I do sincerely hope that they can hold their place with dignity. Meantime, and thank goodness, I still have my memories.

CHAPTER SIX

The Way to the Stars

If Fratton Park was the stage on which my outdoor entertainment was set, the choice of indoor venues was far greater and of infinite variety. Portsmouth was always cinema mad. During those impressionable, formative, juvenile and teenage years of the Thirties and Forties there were more than 30 cinemas in the city. And they offered far more than two films, a newsreel and a trailer. They were centres of social life, a private place in the dark for harmless sexual foreplay and the occasional experiment. They were fashion houses where we digested the latest sartorial ideas from Hollywood, kept a close eye on hair styles ahd picked up the hippest gems of American slang.

Frequently, visits to the pictures constituted a communal exercise, whereby six or eight of us would descend noisily into the stalls for an evening of mayhem. Our attention span and reactions varied according to the entertainment on offer. Ribaldry was reserved for ludicrous Biblical epics, science fiction howlers and varying kinds of British "B" movies. *David and Bathsheba,* for instance, enriched our vocabulary with its stilted transatlantic Bible-speak. Many months after viewing the film, my friend Clive and I were still telephoning each other and as soon as the receiver was lifted it would be a race to inquire: "What of Uriah the Hittite?" If we met in the street, Clive would grab my collar and declare with passionate intensity: "Bathsheba shall not die!" George Pal's sci-fi nonsense *When Worlds Collide,* also sparked our derision. In the film, the planet Bellus was rushing towards earth on an unstoppable collision course. Thereafter, when any of my crowd of mates was asked the time of day, the reply was always this immortal line from the screen-play: "It is ten days to Bellus. There is no error." All quite ridiculous, no doubt, and not too hilarious in print but, at the time, these magical lines would unfailingly reduce us to hysterics.

The supporting British "B" films were notable for the impression they gave of being produced for a sum not exceeding £5. The Edgar Lustgarten crime cases and the Edgar Wallace series were given a rough ride. So, too, were many modest melodramas, often starring an American actor on his inexorable journey down the ladder of fame. We must have infuriated numerous patrons by shouting out the next line of predictable dialogue or substituting it with a better version of our own. We became obsessed with matching up the furniture, wall paintings, lighting fixtures and clothes which would reappear in different locations in a film, occasionally in another film entirely. We were also very keen on night club scenes. The premises, always managed by a dodgy foreigner, were sparsely decorated and populated by "starlets" low on acting ability but presumably high on availability. The customers drank colourless liquid or danced to the urgent rhythms of a brass-filled big band, as the camera panned slowly round a desultory group of four of five musicians on the pocket-sized bandstand. We loved night club sequences.

The kind of movie you'd seen could profoundly affect your mood and behaviour on leaving the cinema. A gangster film, particularly of the *"film noir"* genre, might find you emerging warily from the rear emergency exit to slink cautiously along the pavement. As you slid from shadow to shadow, you were on the watch for fast-approaching cars and listening out for footsteps that stopped when you did. A great musical discharged you into the street buoyant and full of hope for the future as you sang and cavorted down the middle of the road. A tear-jerking love story gave a decided fillip to your own romantic intentions. The girl by your side would be more amenable to a slow amble, the long way home, and with your arm around her waist you might stop to snatch the occasional kiss in a darkened shop doorway. Or light two cigarettes at once and share the moon and stars.

Of course, cinemas varied enormously in ambience and certainly affected one's conduct and disposition. The swish Odeon at North End, which opened in 1936 and to which I was taken by my parents, positively demanded a sober demeanour and attention to the screen. The manager, whose suits were made by my father, would always dash out of his office to greet us, gushing volubly and giving off waves of overpowering scent. As he hovered about us in the foyer, complete with immaculate dinner jacket and bow tie, he had the irritating habit of tweaking my nose between his finger and thumb. More annoying still, he invariably addressed me as "Robin." Whether this represented some wish fulfilment on his part I was too young then to conjecture but a "Robin" I was not, and the regular visit to his office to examine the latest picture stills from Hollywood only partially mollified me.

I couldn't understand why the manager drooled over "divine Nova Pilbeam" and "heavenly Leslie Howard," much preferring the menacing James Cagney or square-shooting Gene Autry. Our host was positively unhinged when *"Gone With the Wind"* arrived. The gleaming black shoes hardly touched the disinfected tiling as we entered the foyer. "You'll love it, love it," he purred, "though" – and I clearly remember his stage whisper to my mother as we climbed the stairs to the Circle – "some of it might be a little beyond Robin." Well, he was right enough, there. I thought it was wet.

Despite the 2,000-seat capacity of this and other cinemas, the late Thirties and Forties were the years of the long wait. Week-ends were especially irksome for it was commonplace to find huge queues on either side of the entrance snaking back down the road and around the corner. With the programmes being continuous, there was no guarantee that the end of the picture would result in an exodus from the one-and-nines. There were tearful occasions when we failed to get in at all, the outcome being an early bedtime and juvenile tantrums.

Cinema architecture varied enormously. The mock Grecian decor of the Regent at North End contrasted violently with the decadence of The Shaftesbury in Kingston Road, which was always an attraction during school holidays. On a wet, boring day it was just possible to fit in three visits to the cinema, with judicious planning and a packet of sandwiches for lunch. The Shaftesbury usually featured long-running serials together with two full-length, if dated, movies. It was here that the ancient "H" (Horror) films came to die and it was only on these occasions that the place would be packed. This could be a problem, for the auditorium was liberally dotted with pillars, many of them in the middle of rows, and it was possible to pass a miserable three hours behind one picking up a satisfactory level of sound but only about 30 per cent. of the picture.

The Plaza, at Bradford Junction, was doubly distinctive. It was so constructed that the queueing hordes could wait inside the foyer, under cover, and it was the only cinema that offered a row of double seats at the back of the stalls. Young couples vied competitively for them and there was a great deal of backward glancing and changing places as and when the coveted seats became vacant. Once secured, the action on the screen became secondary to that at the rear of the hall. For myself, I particularly regret missing almost the entire showing of Betty Grable's epic, *Mother Wore Tights,* and even today I find that

.....there was no guarantee that the end of the big picture would result in an exodus from the one-and-nines.

old and very familiar films on television contain sequences with which I am totally unfamiliar. If locating an usherette to show you to a seat at the Plaza was an onerous task, this was hardly surprising, for they were wont to congregate by the curtains that were draped behind the back row. Here, they took turns to peer through the folds and shine their torches on to hapless, grappling couples at moments of exquisite embarrassment. When running the gauntlet of the torches became too much for hot-blooded patrons, it was necessary to put Plan B into operation.

Two modest flea pits, the Forum in Stamshaw and the Rex in Fratton Road, showed old or extremely old films and very cheaply. They were usually threequarters empty, despite their minuscule proportions, the balcony consisting of only three or four rows of seats. It was more than likely that if you selected a wet, wintry night and an especially lousy movie, you would have the balcony entirely to yourself. Then you only needed an accommodating girl for company and for a couple of two-shilling tickets you acquired three hours' privacy, warmth and several kinds of entertainment.

Perhaps the most fascinating and idiosyncratic of Portsmouth's cinemas was the Palace in Commercial Road. This curious edifice appeared to have been constructed back-to-front. The pay-box and entrance were virtually level with the pavement on the main road and as you passed through the door into total darkness, a momentary panic surfaced. There was no screen! After a few seconds' adjustment to the gloom you found yourself staring at the audience. The postage-stamp sized screen was behind you and there you were – blocking the view. Actually, it was far more interesting, instructive and enjoyable to watch the patrons. The Palace specialised in naughty films which, in the Forties and Fifties, were totally unerotic "B" productions mostly from France and Sweden. Nevertheless, they were as good as it got in those days and the tiny place was jammed to the doors with sailors, rampant for a flash of tit and bum after agonising weeks or months at sea.

It was difficult to comprehend why they bothered with celluloid images. When the fleet arrived in port, the intelligence was conveyed along the railway system to the furthermost reaches of the U.K. Each train arriving at Portsmouth and Southsea station or the harbour would disgorge countless young females intent on a good time, the replenishment of their finances and even marriage. They scurried into the city centre, permed and perfumed, all carrying small square cases crammed with toilet necessities and a change of underwear. Many of them headed directly for the Palace, where the sex-starved ratings were ensconced like so many sitting ducks. Whatever the film, it was never as hot as the floor show!

CHAPTER SEVEN

Cosy Nostra

I have always wanted my own gang. Having no brothers or sisters, heavily influenced by Richmal Crompton's *William* books, the schoolboy camaraderie exemplified in the pages of *Hotspur, Wizard, Adventure* and *Rover,* and by film series featuring the East Side Kids and Andy Hardy, I luxuriated in the company of kindred spirits. Gradually, my little teenaged group evolved with a core of half-dozen regulars and several casual fellow travellers who changed with the seasons. Looking back, I wonder whether the others were actually aware that they belonged to a gang at all. Perhaps they were just very close friends totally oblivious to the organisation that existed in my head or to the machinations necessary to keep the squad intact. Perhaps, but it is gratifying to ponder that, nearly forty years on, most of them are close friends still. Some of us meet rarely but when we do, the years between are as nothing and we pick up the threads in an instant. There is no point in artifice for we knew each other way-back-when. The warmth and affection is mutual, genuine and hopefully, life-lasting.

Though five of us lived within the same square mile, I saw more of Bud than the others. He was our Clark Gable, to whom he bore a passing resemblance. Strong and silent, he rarely essayed a lengthy sentence, preferring a few gruff, *sotto voce* epithets that conveyed his meaning perfectly. Bud was really rather shy except, strangely, in the company of girls where he was given to much eye flashing and outbursts of manic, staccato laughter followed by the devastating smile that usually clinched his success. These rare animated signs of life were invariably accompanied by sundry volatile movements whereby his arms would wave about in short, spastic gestures of no special significance. Tired from such demanding activity, Bud would swiftly relapse into his more familiar somnolence, preferring to lie around looking desirable. Though how he or any of us could look desirable in the clothes we wore in the late Forties is beyond understanding.

There wasn't any style in those days. You grew up wanting to dress like your father's generation and, in any case, that's all there was available. The blazer and grey flannels of the school term gave way to the sober, crumpled suit or sports jacket and flannels of the holidays. And, of course, a tie was *de rigeur.* Bud, being tallish and thin, looked a little better than most of us in his omnipresent chequered sports jacket but strove mightily to destroy this vision with his walk, which was a sort of slouching crawl. Head lowered, shoulders hunched, fists pushed far down into trouser pockets, he would creep along the pavement, face set into an expression of doleful resignation. Even playing football or tennis, he would utilise the minimum of effort most effectively, opting to spread the ball around the field and let the other fools chase it. His tennis serve was a poem in lethargy. A short toss of the ball into the air, the racket thrusting up vertically with no back swing and a stabbing thwack to follow that thoroughly disconcerted his opponents. Bud was no

The gang – Rick, the author, Clive, Bud, Roger, Will – July, 1953

scholar but no fool, either. He operated methodically within his abilities, got drunk very quietly, wooed his women effectively on the dance floor, legs jerking about the arena like a wind-up tin soldier and was a steadfast, loyal friend.

Will – or "Chief" as we called him, God knows why – was a curious bloke. Basically intelligent with a fine mind, he did his best to disguise the fact by acting like a berk most of the time. Will jumped around a lot, making imaginary catches on the boundary, lofting sixes into the pavilion or smashing service aces down the centre line. Slim and loose-jointed, he appeared to move in several directions at once, always noisily. Hardly ever quiet, a mine of useless titbits and forever stirring the rest of us into verbal or physical retaliation, he became marginally worse in the company of girls. Growing more insane by the moment, the welter of vocal scribble was not enhanced by the popping eyes, the slightly protruding teeth and an accompanying fleck or two of froth at the corners of the mouth.

Will's striking rate with females wasn't high, despite his efforts to appear racy and raffish. On dates, his usual rumpled gear was replaced by a suave brown corduroy jacket with a flowing coloured handkerchief in the breast pocket and, the ultimate in chic, a yellow silk scarf which was forever ending up under one ear as he leapt and cavorted. Will and I passed hour upon hour playing a ferociously competitive game of penny football with a ruler and coins on a table top. Throughout, he gave an endless stream of commentary on each match at the top of his voice. He noted the results in a book and would constantly remind me if he had won the last "Cup" by flashing scores at me during the week. He got drunk very easily, though it was difficult to ascertain any particular alteration in his behaviour except that he was liable to fall down rather more often. Will danced like a boxer, perpetually bobbing and weaving, blathered away at the poor girl in his arms and trod on everything and everyone except the floor. He was given, in his few serious moments, to spouting a lot of left-wing political claptrap that he had incorrectly ingested from his sister but none of us paid any attention. He was an invaluable member of the gang, a constant source of merriment and hilarity and a great companion.

Rick was our voice of sanity. Cursed with a deep-seated sense of fair play, his reactions to some of our more outlandish behaviour served as an infallible guide to their acceptability. The gentle remonstrations, sometimes even the unspoken but obvious disapproval of unruly or boorish conduct, usually mine, kept our boisterousness within tolerable bounds. Straight backed, above medium height, darkly handsome and with a ready smile enhanced by a vast array of flashing dentistry, Rick seemed ideally suited to an heroic setting. He was the captain on the bridge of the sinking ship, the matador in the bullring, even Gary Cooper in *Beau Geste*.

He was a magnificent sprinter on the track, and he and I shared a deep and passionate love for that greatest of games, cricket. After the war, Hampshire were not one of the strongest counties but we relished the batting exploits of Arnold, Rogers, Gray and McCorkell and were cheered by the valiant bowling of Shackleton, Knott and Cannings. We marvelled, too, at the accomplishments of Leo Harrison, the only county wicket-keeper to play in spectacles.

Rick dressed, as may be expected, in sober fashion. He usually wore a black blazer, grey flannels, white shirt and striped tie, and his clean-cut appearance served him well with the girls, who were more than flattered to receive such courteous and caring attention. As a result, he was rather more successful socially than I and, I suspect, scored fairly heavily with the ladies. An added bonus was Rick's mastery of all the ballroom dances – most of us hated dancing and did so only as a means of getting our hands on a female – and he shone, particularly, at the tango. The adoration in the eyes of many a local nymphet after she had been swept around the hall in the arms of Pompey's own Fred Astaire was proof that Rick had done his homework. And he could hold his booze. He sank just as much as the rest of us but I never once saw him crash into the furniture.

Every so often, he would disappear for a few weeks without any prior announcement

Roger's imitations were meticulous. This one is Robert Mitchum.

Tarzan (Clive) loves Jane (Thelma).

but there was no cause for alarm. A crowd of us might be sitting drinking in the Cambridge or the Still and West one night when the double-doors would open dramatically and a set of flashing choppers would pierce the blackness. Rick had returned to the fold and, as usual, there was a new, attractive lady on his arm. A sly boots, that lad.

Clive should have had it made. He was very tall, very dark and very handsome. If his morality had matched Erroll Flynn's he would be a sated physical wreck today. Such is the fickleness of Mother Nature, however, that Clive was totally honest, decent and honourable. When he fell in love, which was often, the astonished recipient of his adulation was placed on a pedestal and worshipped from below by her suffering minion. Then it was a bunch of flowers, a box of chocolates, a walk around the cathedral and a kiss on the hand for the lucky lady. It served no purpose to discuss Clive's love life with him for the exercise became much too heart-rending and soul-searing. We let him get on with his scarifying experiences, for we were usually sufficiently agonized about our own, despite his obvious need of sympathy and reassurance.

Along with his other physical attributes, Clive was a magnificent athlete – indeed, he and Rick were both champion sprinters in the county – and he spent much of his time in a tracksuit. In those days tracksuits were a rare species, so Clive's little black number, topped by a military beret, made him an awesome sight as he doubled along the pavement in the early hours. When he was in training he would end his run at my home, where he'd show up about 7 a.m. complete with breakfast – a raw egg and a straw with which to extract the contents.

Entirely lovable and good natured at all times, Clive was also excruciatingly funny. Blessed with total recall, he could recount any event or conversation which of itself was unexceptional but which became increasingly hilarious as he assumed the mien, visage and speech patterns of each person involved, making side-splitting comedy from ordinary behaviour. His eagle eye and sharp ear missed nothing and this facility to replicate details and minutiae were a formidable addition to his artistic talents. Wherever he went, Clive carried a piece of wood and a penknife. He would whittle away for hours, days, weeks, producing marvellous carvings with intricate decoration and would start chopping away at a new chunk of wood as soon as the last was completed. In later life he became a highly skilled potter, worker in metals and sculptor, as well as a noted wood carver.

Like Rick, Clive was a talented dancer and they often hunted in tandem. Much of their tricky terpsichore would be displayed at the Savoy ballroom or at the occasional dances put on at the Oddfellows' Hall in Kingston Road. A rumba, tango or paso doble invariably emptied the floor of all the gropers and stumblers, leaving only the skilled artisans. Clive and Rick worked up a routine whereby, having selected a suitable girl as partner, each would commence dancing at the exact same moment on opposite sides of the floor. They would then go through their pre-rehearsed programme, duplicating each other's steps with perfect timing. Eventually, they would be the only two couples still dancing and their performance always caused a stir, the onlookers unable to understand how apparent strangers could produce identical routines, simultaneously.

It was a relief to come upon something Clive couldn't do. He couldn't drink. He tried, though. Often. Every time, he managed to get as far as the second half-pint of bitter before falling over. Most of our Friday night tours of the pubs ended the same way. We would carry Clive back to my home and my mother would pour black coffee down him until there were signs of life. His return to consciousness was always accompanied by a state of abject contrition for his vile behaviour. He apologised to my parents, to me, to the gang, anybody, innumerable times: "I'm sorry. I'm really sorry. I'm so, so sorry. I'll tell you this – it won't happen again. Never again. Never!" And it didn't. Not till the following Friday.

Every pack has a joker, every group an oddball. Roger was ours. Maybe it was because he was an artist that he saw life through a distorting mirror and lived out flights of fancy that were beyond the ken of we ordinary blokes. A talented painter, Roger was, above all, a brilliant cartoonist and we were convinced that he was destined to join Disney Studios at the earliest opportunity. He certainly worked hard at the artistic temperament and was given to real or self-induced moods of elation, depression, conviviality or total withdrawal. Jolly and cheerful in the morning, he could be, inexplicably, in the dumps after lunch, detonated by a word, a gesture or a whim. He might then disappear for several days or several weeks but would always return in good humour, eventually.

Of medium height and slight build with a cheeky, quizzical expression, he would chip away at everyone with deadly accuracy, deflating our pomposities before sidling off home with his Pompey sailor's roll. His imitations were meticulous and he could transmogrify his voice, face and body into a startling facsimile of such disparate personalities as Robert Mitchum and Toulouse Lautrec. Like any true artist, his clothes betrayed his eccentricity. Faced with the poverty-stricken choice of styles and colours in men's clothes just after the war and a perpetual lack of funds, Roger solved the problem by appropriating some of his mother's wardrobe. A pink cardigan here, blue chiffon scarf there and a variety of colourful accessories placed him at one remove from the grey proletariat. If this suggests that Roger was effete, destroy that thought, for he was a No. 1 Grade A terror with the ladies and had more success than the rest of us put together. Somehow, that perky face and the naughty twinkling eyes proved irresistible and maidens fell hard, fast and often.

Like the rest of the gang, many girls must have been astonished by the frequent changes in persona affected by Roger. Not content with merely borrowing clothes, he introduced more radical changes to his appearance, acquiring a variety of hats, make-up, spectacles, wigs, walking sticks, moustaches and a set of hideously misshapen false teeth. One morning, I opened the front door to confront a wizened Indian in a turban, begging for money. Thus attired, Roger lived the role for some days, creating havoc wherever he went. He caused similar consternation among shop assistants all over Portsmouth as an ultra-finicky dandy, complete with white flannels, striped blazer, straw hat, cane and monocle.

.....Roger suddenly flung himself head first into a privet hedge.

Having fun – 1952 style. Shirley, Rick, Thelma, Roger, the author, Will, Bunty, Clive, John, Bud.

Once, strolling along Kirby Road chatting casually with him, I was transfixed as Roger suddenly flung himself head first into a privet hedge. He emerged from the other side grinning and badly scratched, explaining that his idea had been to test the reactions of passers-by to this odd happening. In the event, there wasn't a soul around but me, though Roger declared complete satisfaction with the experiment. On another occasion, I was walking home about midnight and came across what appeared to be a tramp lying in the gutter. As I hurried past, an unmistakable voice, strangulated by uncontrollable laughter emanated from the tawdry heap: "Shirley sends her love and says she'll meet you outside the gents' lavatory at 8 o'clock." Shirley was my current girl friend – and you've guessed the rest. Actually, Roger even tried lying in the middle of the road – the main A3 at North End, no less, with its teeming traffic – "just to see if anyone would stop." No-one did.

If Roger ever got drunk I didn't notice and in the light of the strangeness of his "normal" behaviour, it would have been impossible to detect, anyway. His range of moods and personality changes was bewildering but enormous fun. A genuine nutcase, he enriched our lives and gave pleasure to us all.

These five – Bud, Will, Rick, Clive and Roger – were the members of my gang. I was the unofficial organiser responsible for getting and keeping us together, fixing up some lively socialising and providing a regular meeting place. In the event, it was logical that our headquarters should be my house. My parent's house, that is. It was understood, in the telepathic, unspoken acknowledgement prevalent in a group of close-knit youngsters, that everyone gravitated, eventually, to 24, Kirby Road. Conveniently so, for it was a large house and I could easily manipulate my mother, father and grandmother into the dining room while the mob luxuriated in what my mother called "the lounge." Coffee and biscuits would appear from the kitchen as if by magic, my parents exchanged a few pleasantries and promptly fled from the onslaught of the latest Stan Kenton 78, played at top volume.

The lounge, the radiogram, sofa, comfortable chairs, drinks cabinet, sundry boxes of sweets and chocolates, were all ours. We were still at school and dependent upon the generosity of our parents for pocket money, so poncing on my folks was infinitely preferable to tramping around the pubs of Portsmouth – except at week-ends, of course. If we pooled resources and topped up our modest purchases of beer, cider, port or sherry with a few drams from my Dad's drinks supply, all we needed, then, was the girls. Ah, the girls . . .

Getting our act together – 1953.

CHAPTER EIGHT

Neck and Neck

Like all teenagers, at all times, everywhere, we were obsessed with sex. The trouble was, back in the Forties and early Fifties, sex was just like any one of the many rationed items of the period – there wasn't much of it and what there was was difficult to obtain. Oh, every so often the gates opened and you were offered a glimpse of heaven. Three months' concentrated attention, pictures, restaurants, chocolates, the lot and you might get a handful in the back row of the Odeon. On the outside of her bra, of course. Another few months' graft may give you the courage to plunge a hopeful hand up that seersucker skirt, thrash your way through a dozen petticoats towards the major prize and briefly fondle a dimpled knee. But you rarely, very rarely, got any further. You knew what was there – you'd seen it all in films and magazines – but that delicious band of flesh bulging tantalisingly above the stocking tops was invariably a no-go-area. We lived in hope and, once in a very long while, a couple of us made it past the post but most of us wouldn't have known what to do if the offer was there in writing.

So, failing sex, we contrived to fall in love. Well, I certainly did; I fell in love continually. I was crazy about Doreen, mainly – no, entirely – because of her breasts. She was small and so were they, but it was their shape that fascinated me. They were conical and so exaggerated as to resemble ice-cream cornets. Whether they were real or she had patented her own hoist mechanism I never discovered, though I tried hard enough. As soon as my hand was in range, Doreen would sway backwards, simultaneously cracking me on the wrist with one hand and around my face with the other. "Naughty, naughty," she would chide coyly. Despite the pain, I persevered but she beat me to the draw every time.

I grew wild with desire for her, wrote a series of heartrending "Doreen Poems" extolling her many virtues and presented them to her, laboriously hand-written in elaborate capital letters in a school exercise book. It was fruitless. Her castles remained in the air, unassailed, and gradually my unrequited passion waned. I settled for Yvonne whose bosom was not only larger but more accessible. Indeed, she was perfectly content to lie back on the sofa and let me help myself but each time her dress was unbuttoned and bra removed, the atmosphere instantly became heavy with the odour of mothballs and damp wallpaper. It was too indelicate to inquire as to the exact nature of this groper repellent – perhaps her body was reacting to my assaults in the same manner as a cornered skunk – but it was impossible to work surrounded by such a musty, distracting aroma.

Doris was a doll-faced, sweet natured girl, deliciously soft wherever you touched her but, despite her eager compliance, our affair was ruthlessly destroyed by the transport system. She lived in a railway cottage by Copnor Bridge, a mere couple of yards from the main line. No sooner had we settled on the sofa than a train would roar past, shattering the romantic aura and redistributing the furniture as it hopped and bumped around the room. Ornaments crashed, crockery rattled and it was perfectly possible to get your tongue bitten off as the 10.17 screamed behind your ears. The shocks played hell with your libido, passion dissolved into hysteria and Doris was as safe as the Bank of England.

Valerie was a snooty girl who went to the High School and called me "Darling Boy." She had obviously been groomed for a position of authority and certainly expected to get her way in all things. Whenever I attempted to kiss her, she would throw her arms about me and, in a vice-like grip, bend me backwards at an angle of 45 degrees, just like in the silent movies. As I struggled to stay on my feet, Valerie's tightly closed lips would crash into the approximate area of my mouth. That's when she would always say: "Darling boy, darling boy." I appreciated the sentiment but the bruises took days to fade.

Valerie grew fond of our head banging sessions and finally, I could take no more. I told her that I was in love with someone else. She considered my statement for a few seconds, then began methodically and cold-bloodedly to kick me. This outburst of violence apparently failed to satisfy her and she took to hanging around my house for hours, despite the freezing, snowbound time of year. Whenever I appeared, she would hurl snowballs with stones inside as I ran the gauntlet up the garden path. Growing bolder, she knocked at the front door and when I opened it, unloaded a fusillade of lethal snowballs at my head. One of them struck my father's beloved grandfather clock and smashed the glass face. Tempus failed to fugit for a week or so and Valerie's time was up, too. I hope her husband doesn't wear dentures.

I fell hopelessly and irretrievably for Diana. This was unusual for she was a couple of inches taller than I and that sort of thing always gives me a distinct feeling of inferiority. But she was one of those rare girls who possessed what we, then, called a masculine sense of humour. She was well versed in all the latest Hollywood slang and jazz hip talk, an irresistible combination, and besides, she was very attractive with sensational blue eyes. For a few weeks it was a big, wide, wonderful world and I lived on cloud nine. Then I sensed her growing indifference and Diana would make excuses to break dates. In despair, I started to get drunk a lot and one Friday night at the Savoy Ballroom we had a terrible row. Wildly jealous because she was dancing with the same partner all the time and ignoring me, I waited for the interval. That was when she always took her shoes off to cool her feet and, as she did so, I surreptitiously filled one of them with light ale. I was going to show her how much I loved her by drinking out of her shoe but before I could do so, she slipped her foot back into it. That really cooled her off and she cursed me violently in front of the gang and her new inamorato. Well pissed, humiliated and beyond consolation, I dashed up to the balcony and tried to throw myself out of an open window. Bud, Clive and Rick grabbed me just in time.

After lying awake all night, racked by guilt and remorse, I got up about 5 o'clock and staggered the mile and a half to Diana's home. I sat on the wall outside and waited. At half past seven, her mother opened the front door, saw me but said nothing, picked up the milk and went inside. Frozen and frenzied, I continued my vigil. An hour or so later, Diana came out on to the front doorstep eating a piece of toast and glowering ferociously. I poured my heart out as she nibbled her breakfast unconcernedly. I apologised, grovelled, begged her to give me another chance and promised that our future together would be happy, exciting, fulfilling. I even offered to spend money on her.

"What's your answer, then?" I pleaded. "What's your answer? Is it OK? What do you say? Can we make a fresh start?"

She finished her toast, wiped her hands slowly on her handkerchief and appeared to be giving the matter deep and serious thought.

"Piss off, shitbag," she said.

Her decision seemed to suggest a degree of finality – so I pissed off.

Forty-eight hours later I was terminally in love with Annette. Curiously, this episode was really the Diana debacle in reverse. Annette was a fiery red-headed Irish girl with ambitions to be a nurse. She was deeply religious and Roman Catholic but mostly good fun, nevertheless. My atheistic mutterings and fairly frequent swearing drove her into a constant lather and I was many times burned to a crisp in the eternal fires while my immortal soul took a terrible hammering in whatever infernal region she'd had it consigned. But she forgave my corporate depravities, though it doubtless cost her an inordinate number of hours in confession, and set about my conversion with tireless enthusiasm. I was prepared to suffer her tedious lectures so long as she conjoined with my lecherous intentions when appropriate. But it got to be a bore. I told Annette that enough was enough and she became increasingly distraught, fervently entreating me to recant. After a couple of hysterical hours it was too late and too far gone for any retractions but she was a long, long way from submission.

She took to following me on her bicycle, very slowly and at some distance if I was walking, pedalling like fury and close behind if I was on a bus. It might be cold, raining and blowing a gale out there, as I peered through the misted trolley-bus window, but there she'd be, red hair flying and knees flailing away, chasing me up Fratton Road on her old Raleigh cycle. I began to feel persecuted and panic-stricken, for she always seemed to know when I was leaving my house. She continued to tail me, even when I was with another girl. Then came the awful day. I was sitting upstairs on the bus, in the back seat, mesmerically watching the toiling, sweating figure pedalling in pursuit some thirty yards behind. I looked away for a moment, looked back, and she was gone. She failed to reappear. I was almost worried for, being something of a reactionary, I've always disliked changed circumstances.

Later that evening, I was lying in the long grass on Portsdown Hill with Norma from the newsagent's. She was an entirely oral girl, everything finding its way, eventually, to those generous lips of hers. And it was as well that her mouth was frequently full for she had absolutely nothing to say, being concerned only with her next meal, in whatever form it may take. So there we were on Portsdown Hill, before the city architects replaced its green slopes with a remarkable facsimile of Alcatraz, when Bud appeared, puffing his way up the path. He brought news of Annette. She had fallen off her bicycle, which explained her sudden disappearance, and in falling had contrived to ram the brake lever several inches deep into her thigh. She required some surgery but refused to allow it unless and until I showed up at her bedside. There was even an ambulance waiting at the bottom of the hill to whisk me across to St James's.

I found the poor girl looking stricken with a nasty circular hole in her leg but she brightened as I entered the room. I held her hand while the necessary doctoring was effected, kissed her on the forehead afterwards and left. I never saw Annette again. The front wheel of her bike had radically altered shape and she was in no condition to undertake much exercise for several months. I heard that she became a student nurse and moved to the north of England. I hope she settled in a town without too many hills.

Teenaged girls often hunted in pairs. Invariably, one was attractive, the other not. It's a fair assumption that the pretty one was entirely aware that she looked even more inviting when juxtaposed with her friend and would automatically have first pick of the available males. But her partner's cause was also served for she, at least, was always on hand to make up a foursome and first on the scene to snaffle her friend's cast-offs on the rebound.

As it happened, Bud and I frequently drifted around the city in search of what we called "talent." If the pubs, cafes and sea-front failed to provide any receptive company, we could always call on Anne and Ira, sisters who were generally game for that pastime which was both therapeutic and frustrating, a "necking session." Although their mother was well aware of our intentions, she encouraged our visits, monopolised the conversation and refused to leave us alone. We first thought that this was merely a device to protect her daughters but she soon enthusiastically suggested playing games like postman's knock and insisted on joining in. Bud and I agreed that not only was she

. . . . .all lust dispelled, we stood there incapable of dealing with the problem.

prettier and more stimulating company than Anne and Ira but she kissed better, too. Growing envious of their mother's obvious popularity, the girls ceased to invite us indoors. They invented ludicrous excuses to prevent us calling:

"We've got the decorators in for the next six months":

"A wall has collapsed in the living room":

"We're infested with rats."

And straining desperately for even greater disasters:

"Mum's got piles and it makes her nervous":

"The cat's sick and has to have absolute peace and quiet."

It was a relief to discover Edna and Peggy, another incongruous duo. Edna was a fearsome creature, powerfully built, belligerent, loud-voiced and coarse. One could overlook the deficiencies, however, and the fact that she was addicted to wrestling – during the course of which she regularly drew blood while ending up on top – in view of her quite magnificent chest. Her breasts were not only substantial but had the appearance and consistency of concrete grapefruit. Edna was perfectly happy to have her bosom mauled and would even suggest it, once the wrestling was over. She would then lie catatonically rigid and still, her legs jammed together as if with superglue, while you attended to her orbs. She hoped to join the W.R.N.S. eventually and would surely have proved a formidable addition to the senior service. With her innately ferocious expression and rock-like chest, I imagined her tied to the prow of a battleship.

Despite Edna's dominance, her friend Peggy was no shrinking violet. A beautiful girl with magnificent legs and a lithe athletic body, she was a keen racing cyclist and would practise regularly on the track at Alexandra Park. I lusted after her shamelessly but whenever the four of us settled down to an evening at home, it was always me with Edna and Bud with Peggy for the first half-hour. Thirty minutes with Edna, spent mostly in a half-nelson, took its toll and by the time we changed over partners, I was in no condition to prove to Peggy that she and I were meant for each other.

My erotic fantasies were never fulfilled, the two occasions that I managed to get her to myself being dogged by misfortune. We met on a glorious, if breezy, summer evening and strolled along the sea front. As dusk fell, we settled on to a bench in the Rock Gardens but an increasingly powerful wind blowing in from the ocean caused our undoing. The bench was next to the garden's *chef-d'oeuvre,* an undistinguished but lively fountain with illuminated jets that constantly changed colour. A particularly vicious gust of wind suddenly besieged the fountain and deposited sheets of water over us, as if we were a couple of amorous mongrels in the middle of the main road. All passion died instantly.

Some weeks later I saw Peggy, head down over the handlebars, tearing down the Esplanade near South Parade Pier. After waving her down, we spent a couple of hours until closing time in the Still and West. By then, we were both fairly drunk and Peggy was too unsteady to ride her bike, so we walked the four miles home, stopping every so often to grapple in a darkened shop doorway. I was feeling shattered yet bursting with frustration by the time we had reached Peggy's home in Tipner. We crept into the garage and in parking her racing machine against the wall, dislodged the bicycle pump which fell on to the floor. She and I both bent down to retrieve it. She got there first and in bringing it up off the ground, accidentally rammed one end of it very hard between my legs. Half-an-hour later, long after Peggy had gone indoors, I felt almost well enough to contemplate staggering back to my place.

These juvenile high jinks may lead you to surmise that the Swinging Sixties arrived fifteen years early in Portsmouth, but in truth, sexual intercourse was rarely, very rarely, achieved and hardly ever attempted. The contraceptive pill had yet to make its cataclysmic appearance, so fear held the key. Thus the imagination took over once foreplay reached its physical terminus, leaving one in a ferment of anticipation, hope and ultimately, of ignorance. You've got to do it, to do it! I finally made it in 1947.

About a dozen of us, neatly paired off, were sitting around in the lounge at Kirby Road. Nat "King" Cole's version of "Nature Boy" was weaving its spell on the turntable and there were eight or nine more 78s stacked up on the auto-changer. I was with Joan, who was some ten years older than me, obviously experienced, and she was driving me wild. "Let's go upstairs," I whispered daringly and she immediately concurred. We crept into my bedroom, she lay down on my bed, I clambered on hot with passion and before I could lay a finger on her, had made rather a nasty mess of her dress. Deeply ashamed, I apologised profusely. Joan patted me reassuringly and inquired, very gently: "First time?" I thought about it for a moment but the evidence was overwhelming. I nodded. She smiled and patted me again. "We'll have to see whaat we can do about it," she said with a smile. Over the following few months she gave me an education for which I'm grateful to this day. Wherever Joan is now, I hope she's happy.

Christine was something else entirely. A remote girl, with a thinly veiled sneer of contempt rarely absent from her lips, she was, nevertheless, attractive and highly desirable. Bud, Roger and I met her by chance and she invited us to a late-night party. Arriving at the house about 11 p.m., we discovered that she was its only occupant and that nobody else was expected. Christine left us alone in the dimly lit living room, to return shortly, completely naked. She lay down on the sofa, leant on one elbow and looked quizzically at us. Totally disconcerted, out of our depth and with all lust dispelled, we stood there incapable of dealing with the problem. Eventually, each of us took a dining chair across to the sofa and sat next to her, wondering what to do. Roger, of course, was the first to make a move, running his hands over the reclining nude. Bud joined him and I made a few desultory passes at her legs.

Christine lay there, inert, and plainly disinterested. It was about as sexy as mowing the lawn. After a few minutes of this nonsense, she stood up, brushing away our feeble fingers as if they were cobwebs. "I'm going home," she said. It transpired that the house we were in was her sister's and that Christine lived several miles away, in Cosham. "Who's taking me?" she inquired. She glanced around the room imperiously while we digested the implications. It was late, the last bus had gone, we couldn't afford a taxi, it was raining. She frightened me and I wasn't keen. Roger was keen but didn't fancy the long walk. Bud volunteered, reasoning that it was a question of swings and roundabouts. We met him the following day, dying to know what had happened. "She didn't utter a bloody word all the way home," he said "and when we got to her gate she marched straight up the path and indoors without even a sodding goodnight." The rain had become heavier and Bud was saturated on the return journey. Roger and I congratulated each other on our good fortune. We later heard that Christine had moved to London and went on the game and although we were never able to verify this information it made some kind of sense in the light of our experience. She may well have earned a great deal of money over the years, too, but it won't have been a lot of fun.

Sexy, green-eyed Greta was supposed to be hot stuff, so I asked her for a date. It turned out that she was only interested in eating. Sitting through *Gilda* at the Plaza, in those inviting back row double seats, moreover, she demolished six bars of Fry's Chocolate Cream. Even her hand was too sticky to hold and afterwards, she demanded a meal. I took her to Maxime's, a luxurious establishment opposite the King's Theatre which supplied a generous dinner for 7s.6d. Greta was gloriously sick on the way home, which afforded me some vicarious recompense, but it wasn't worth further outlay to repeat the experience. There was always someone else on hand, however, for Greta very soon became pregnant and, shortly after, married. She must have eaten something that didn't agree with her.

Helen was a beauty, one of the very few Jewish girls with whom I would dare to socialise. She was a splendid jazz singer and possessed that laid back, offbeat sense of humour that jazz people develop instinctively. With us, it was the music that mattered and merely a bonus that she was such a good companion and friend. Going out with Jewish girls was a hazardous venture, usually, fraught with terrifying possibilities. Before you'd brought her home after the very first date, the grapevine would be throbbing with more relevant data about you than could be crammed into the most sophisticated computer. That you were unlikely to become a member of the holy trinity – a doctor, lawyer or accountant – weighed heavily against you but such was a mother's urgent desire to get her daughter safely married off before she was left on the shelf at the advanced age of twenty, you could be guaranteed serious consideration, providing you weren't a convicted murderer.

If you took a Jewish girl out twice you were really in trouble, as this was tantamount to a declaration of eternal fidelity. Mother and daughter would go looking for engagement rings, father wanted to know how much you earned, how much your father earned, what were your prospects. The wedding invitation list was in its first round of preparation. Next came the summons to dinner; if you went, it was *mazeltov* and goodnight. If you didn't, the entire congregation would be made aware that you were a double-dyed bastard. Suddenly, your parents are asked to tea, treated like rich relatives and the bargaining begins. When you call for the third date, you find that it's all decided. You're engaged. There's a bonus – you get your first kiss.

From then on, you observe helplessly from the sidelines. The wedding invitations are printed, 350 for her family and 25 for yours. The merry-go-round picks up speed. You discover that your parents are in league with her parents. Your future is mapped out for the next twenty-five years, your bank account is changed into joint names. Tomorrow, they'll show you the flat they've found for you, just around the corner from her parents. They'll find you a better job, too. And sell you their second car, cheap. You realise that you've seen far more of the parents than the daughter, but after all, you're one of the family now. There's a silver lining, of course. Next week, it's the wedding and you're due for that second kiss. What I really mean to say is that, mercifully, it wasn't like that with Helen. She was a friend.

In no way friendly was Brenda, who lived in Copnor Road and terrorised all the young males in the area. Appropriately named "Tiger" because of her wild behaviour, Brenda had long, frizzy hair that sprang from her head like a startled ginger bush and was entirely in accord with her character. She was obsessed by boys, whom she sought to dominate by battering into submission. Forever on watch through an upstairs window, she scanned Copnor Road and College Park opposite for fresh meat, rushing out of the house as soon as some was sighted. An ululating scream provided the only warning you were likely to get that Brenda was bearing down upon you at speed and that's exactly how I was trapped, after several hours of exhausting tennis in the park. There was no escape. We had met only briefly, at a party, but she greeted me with paralysing thumps on the back and punches on the upper arm that sent shock waves down to my feet.

The Tiger was a skinny, not especially good-looking girl with piercing green eyes that scanned your face perpetually for the slightest indication of encouragement. Not that reticence discouraged her for the pummelling was habitually followed by an excruciatingly painful and violent attack that was Brenda's version of a kiss. Grabbing a handful of hair, she snapped my head backwards and sank her teeth into my lower lip, drawing blood and ricking my neck simultaneously. Those teeth-jarring experiences with "darling boy" Valerie were exquisitely tender by comparison. The Tiger's vampiric tendencies were well-known in the district and may have caused many a youth to take up smoking. Having a fag in your mouth gave you, at least, a few seconds respite before the fangs were bared.

Brenda wasn't interested in any kind of physical response from the boys she devastated but she always demanded verbal assurances of total adoration.

"Tell me you love me. Tell me, tell me," she bellowed.

"I love you, Brenda," I mumbled. It wasn't good enough.

"TELL me," she shrieked. Her cat's eyes bore into mine, tearing me to shreds.

"I love you," I repeated, somewhat more fervently, aware that having destroyed my mouth, she was quite likely to sink her incisors into an ear. She smiled radiantly at my admission and contented herself with a short right jab to the solar plexus, while rubbing her Brillo pad of hair back and forth on my cheek. A final punch between the shoulder blades indicated her satisfaction and imminent departure. "See you then," she bawled, wheeling away suddenly and breaking into a run back towards her lair. I don't know if Brenda ever married, but I'd know her husband anywhere. He would be the one with cauliflower ears and lips like chewed string.

My affair with Mary was one of those drawn-out on/off romances that should have been laid to rest at the first "off," but which we both contrived to prolong. A sweet-natured, very pretty and lovable girl, she brought out the best and the worst in me. She made me care and want to protect her but her passivity gradually induced me to take advantage of her. After the third or fourth break-up and reconciliation, it became for me a relationship that was convenient rather than necessary and was punctuated by episodes that displayed my unattractive and escalating lack of respect for her.

Without doubt, I treated Mary shabbily from time to time and my mother grew increasingly exasperated by my behaviour. When I casually mentioned that I was going to London for the week-end to stay with another girl, my mother dashed into the lavatory, had hysterics and refused to come out until I promised that I would stay in Portsmouth with Mary. Faced with such a threat, I felt that my only recourse was to accede to her wishes but some time later realised that I had been conned. Why should it matter whether my mother stayed in the lavatory or not? It didn't affect me either way – we had another loo downstairs – and it had absolutely no relevance to my relationship with Mary. That's mothers for you, though. They know their sons backwards, forwards and sideways and they always win. Well, Jewish mothers do.

The reactions of Mary's mother were interesting, too. She had never really accepted me, anyway, but at one stage had told her daughter: "You're not going to marry a Jewish pig." (Now there's a contradiction in terms). The final outcome has caused me to smile many times, albeit a trifle sadistically. Mary married a German.

With almost every group of young males there are one or two girls who become tacitly accepted as members, without any sort of discussion or majority consent. Thelma, an intelligent, truly beautiful girl with a sunny nature and bubbling sense of humour was not really a member at all but simply joined the crowd from time to time. We all liked her immensely, we all thought she looked sensational, we all fell in love with her and a couple of us went out with her. But it was always a platonic thing with Thelma and for my own part, I suffered a complete loss of nerve where she was concerned and could never ask her for a date. Not that it would have made any difference, for she had been in love with the same boy since her schooldays. As it turned out, she had unerringly found the right partner at the outset and she is still happily married to him. And still very beautiful.

Bunty was our true sister confessor and undoubtedly one of the gang. Easy going, untroubled, very attractive and ever ready to laugh, she moved and spoke in a lazy, casual manner that was relaxing and reassuring. She was on our wavelength and usually accompanied us on most of our less sordid forays. With her undemanding friendliness, Bunty swiftly became loved and respected by us all and although most of us took her out singly on occasion, there never seemed to be any possibility of reckless passion fouling up our relationship with her. I supposed that she would eventually drift away, find her niche and her man. I was wrong. Bunty stayed – and married Will.

CHAPTER NINE

Shouldering Arms

So we passed or failed our final exams and came to face what we dreaded most. National Service. There was no avoiding it, for we could all breathe and walk and none of us had influence in high places. Thus, we were stuck with an unwelcome two-year hiatus in our lives and went our various ways into the Army or the R.A.F. I didn't expect to enjoy it but I didn't bargain for an experience that, after so many years, still rates as the most miserable time of my life. The Army method was very simple. It systematically destroyed you as a human being and then rebuilt you in its own image. In service terms, it made a man of you, though what kind of man is a matter worthy of discussion elsewhere. Everyone has a fund of National Service stories and, by now, everyone has written about them, so the subject will receive mercifully short shrift here. Still, one or two anecdotes might strike a few chords and in any case, I shall feel better for having told you.

Our corporal, a totally unprincipled bully with minimal intelligence who frankly admitted deriving much pleasure from terrorising conscripts, harangued us with the usual selection of well-worn insults. You know the sort of thing:

"How tall are you, son?"

"Five foot nine, corporal."

"I never knew they piled shit so high."

My platoon sergeant crystallized matters perfectly, at church parade on the very first Sunday:

"On my command, C. of E.s take three paces forward, R.C.s take three paces backwards, wogs stand where you are."

I was discovered to be the only wog. The ignorant mass of humanity, mostly from the mean streets of Glasgow and London, now had an outlet for their spleen and someone upon whom to vent their frustration for the humiliation and viciousness that they themselves were enduring. They were enthusiastically backed up by assorted trained soldiers (regulars), and N.C.O.s. Thus, the platoon Jew was beaten up, given the dirtiest jobs and had his kit or personal belongings defaced and stolen. I returned from duty one evening to find my bed missing. It had been dismantled and spread to all parts of the camp, along with the shredded bedding. I could, maybe should, have gone to authority and complained but public schoolboys don't do that. Fortunately, after basic training had been completed, I managed to get home to Portsmouth most week-ends by the simple expedient of bribing my sergeant. Ten shillings bought me a 36-hour pass, £1 entitled me to 48 hours. It was worth every penny, though my pay was a mere 28 shillings a week.

I gained further respite by enrolling for a four-month shorthand and typing course, but first, I was required to attend a W.O.S.B. The W.O.S.B. (War Office Selection Board) was a four-day course for potential officers. A potential officer was anyone who went to a public or grammar school or was born into the privileged echelons of society, and such people were automatically listed to attend at Barton Stacey, in Hampshire. I had no real wish to be an officer but the lure of four days' civilised treatment, reasonable food and uncrowded living accommodation was too strong to refuse.

Regrettably, the company was, in its way, as unpleasant and ignorant as the moronic hordes I'd left behind in camp, containing a great many snobbish, bigoted boors who all seemed to be called Piers, Rollo or Toby. The air rang with their shrill laughter and cries of "I say, look here!" Each evening, groups of these hoorays milled about Barton Stacey, instantly recognisable even in civvies by the way they slicked down their hair in the wrong direction across their foreheads. These upper class twits were on to a good thing, as the regular officers who were conducting the tests and interviews and, indeed, selecting the successful W.O.S.B. candidates, were frequently products of the very same public schools. At Portsmouth Grammar, the sixth forms comprised those who studied the sciences, the arts, the classics, or economics. The residue were shuffled into Services Sixth and it was from this bunch of thickies that a quantity of regular officers emerged in the Army – the last refuge of the privileged idiot. All this might go a long way to explain our stainless military heritage and the glories of Empire.

For me, The W.O.S.B. was a four-day farce. Throughout, the object was to catch the eye and ear of the adjudicators. Group discussions on a variety of instantly selected topics degenerated into a Babel of incomprehensible gibberish, the successful member being the one who could monopolise the occasion by talking longer and louder than his fellows. The intelligence tests included written and outdoor exercises. For the latter, half a dozen of us would be placed on a raised platform, given a couple of large logs, some

I considered my two years of National Service were entirely barren and pointless.

iron bars and a length of rope and told to move to another raised platform about ten yards away without touching the ground in between. This resolved into the usual verbal dogfight to determine who among us had the most stunningly original idea for achieving the aerial journey. I suggested pole vaulting with an iron bar but was instantly crushed by snorts of derision. I lost interest, thereafter.

My fate was sealed at the interview. The major conducting this lunacy was a supercilious, pompous blimp, archetypally replete with an excruciatingly affected accent and built-in sneer. He left me in no doubt as to the outcome of our meeting:

"Your father's a tailor, I see."

"Yes, sir."

"Your surname. Is it, er, foreign?"

"Polish I think, sir."

"Hmmm. None of your people in the services, I suppose?"

"No, sir. Not since the war."

"Yes, well, your sort don't take to the life as a rule, do they?"

"What sort is that, sir?"

The major turned a delicate shade of puce, cleared his throat noisily and shot me a look of undisguised loathing. He changed tack:

"Why do you want to be an officer?"

I'd had enough of this crap:

"More money, sir."

I failed the W.O.S.B.

Back in camp, at Aldershot, I commenced my shorthand and typing course, looking forward to a period of relative calm. At the final exams, I passed the typing test fairly comfortably and secured a good shorthand result by cheating. I made a deal with the lad sitting next to me whereby he took down one half of a sentence and I grappled with the other half. In this way, by copying each other's work surreptitiously, we both doubled our shorthand speed.

I cherish one gloriously joyful memory of these doomy days. Our Company was due to play another, at cricket. This was a serious matter to our superiors and they scoured the ranks for talent. There was very little available and when it was discovered that I had led my school team, I was appointed captain and made responsible for the composition of the side that would uphold the Company's honour. As we emerged from the pavilion on the great day, my platoon second lieutenant, a typically ineffectual nit, could not bear to cede his authority to an Other Rank, even on the cricket field. "Look here," he said, "I'll take over the captaincy. More my line of work than yours." Before I could answer, he bounded ahead, clapping his hands and shouting: "Come on, chaps. Let's sort out the positions." I was quite a speedy bowler and my leader graciously tossed me the ball and set an attacking field, with himself the second of three slips. My first two balls were wides. The third was a fast full toss which the batsman slashed at, hard. It went like a rocket towards the slips. "Mine!" screamed our captain, and it certainly was. The ball ripped through his limply cupped hands and smashed into his groin, whereupon he emitted an agonised "Aargh" and subsided gracefully backwards on to the turf. Several grinning squaddies ran on and bore the punctured pillock away to the M.O., while I resumed the leadership, lost the match and somehow acquired six extra cookhouse fatigues. It was worth every mud-caked potato and greasy tureen.

My miserable days effectively ended when I was transferred to the Intelligence Corps depot at Uckfield, in Sussex. Within a week I was sent to join a Field Security Section at Wilton, near Salisbury, where the lack of a real war and genuine spies to interrogate reduced activities, as far as I was concerned, to the sort of games kids play. The section dashed about the area investigating disaffected soldiers who said nasty things about royalty, checked on suspected Communists, hunted down saboteurs who put sand in petrol tanks and made sure that secret documents weren't left lying around in officers'

"Why do you want to be an officer?"

lavatories. It all made little sense to me but, in truth, I'd long since given up on the Army and in any case, my job was merely a clerical and administrative one. The routine was broken by jolly jaunts into the countryside, known as manoeuvres, where we slept in trucks or haystacks for a week or two and pretended to be at war.

The last six months of my service were enlivened by the affair with Jackie. Merely recalling the manner of our meeting can still bring me out in a sweat. I had just completed 14 days' detention for arriving back an hour late from a week-end at home. Feeling lonely and depressed I took a bus into Salisbury to see Mario Lanza in *The Great Caruso*. Utterly bored by the mind-numbing banality of the film, I tried, for the first and only time in my life, to pick up a girl in the cinema. Sitting next to me in the semi-dark, I could just make out an attractive profile set off by a cheeky bubble-cut hair style. Her left hand rested on her thigh and I gradually inched my fingers across and on top of hers. I was powerless to stop myself and in a fervid state of excitement and apprehension. I expected the girl to leap to her feet screaming and my mind raced ahead anticipating awful public and military repercussions.

But she didn't move or speak and let my hand remain on hers. After an agonising few minutes, I stroked her knuckes gently and to my amazement, she reciprocated, turning her hand and sliding her fingers through mine. I was almost delirious with the daring of it all and my apparent success. We remained unmoving and without looking at each other until Lanza had burst his final blood vessel and the lights went up. She smiled at me, which made her look even prettier. Then she stood up and to my horror seemed to be at least six feet two. Certainly, she was almost six inches taller than I and that, of course, not only embarrassed me but seriously undermined my confidence. Standing on tiptoe, I reluctantly offered to walk her home. We exchanged names while Jackie and I assured one another that we had never behaved in such a manner before. She, too, was away from home and lonely, which was probably why she had deigned to trifle with a midget. An unhappy love affair had driven her to enlist in the W.R.A.C. and thus began my only meaningful relationship with a second lieutenant. Jackie was a sweet girl and brought much pleasure into an unhappy period of my life. We didn't go out much though. At least, not in the daylight.

While admitting to a jaundiced attitude, not entirely based on my unfortunate experiences, I considered my two years of National Service were entirely barren and pointless. If you are in any way a nonconformist or possess a degree of individuality, the services are not for you. I found the conscripted army, like the regular army, to be a haven for moronic, effete upper-class berks and moronic, sadistic lower-class nerks and the system provided the perfect setting for each to prosper, not only without let or hindrance but even, sadly, with encouragement. I sincerely hope things have changed for the better.

CHAPTER TEN

Junk Man

During 1952/53, the gang gradually filtered back to base and came to grips with the problem of earning a living. Portsmouth's vast Dockyard offered scope to those of us with technical resources. Will went into the Civil Service and Roger set about deploying his artistic talents. I tried to get a job with the Portsmouth Evening News, rather fancying myself as the ace reporter, but there were no vacancies. While playing football in the Army, a couple of scouts from Third Division clubs had approached me with offers of a trial. I'd never thought about playing football professionally but if I did, it could only be for Pompey.

I presented myself at Fratton Park and after leaping about on the turf for twenty minutes was put into several trial matches. My lasting memory of these debacles is of nervously going forward to tackle the Scottish international full-back, Alex Wilson, as he thundered towards me. He hit me admidships and disappeared over the horizon with the ball, leaving me shattered in a pool of mud. After my final game, I was summoned to the office of manager, Bob Jackson. "Lad," he said, one hand on my shoulder, "you will never be a professional as long as you've got a hole in your arse." I gave his delicate judgment my full consideration. If he knew me that intimately after such a brief association, he must surely be right. I retired to the calmer waters of the Sunday and Midweek leagues where the pace was slower, the opposition less terrifying, and managed to enjoy the sport until the age of forty-six. Then a tackle, similar to that of Alex Wilson's, convinced me that it was time to hang up my jockstrap.

I prepared to launch myself upon the waiting business world, my only pressing decision being upon whom to bestow my many and varied talents. While recognising the necessity of securing gainful employment, I reserved my enthusiasm and dedication for the hobbies and pastimes that really interested me – sport, girls and jazz. Music remains an indestructible passion in my life. Since the age of six, when I came across a pile of old 78s in the junk room at home, I have been consumed not merely by the sounds contained within the grooves but the very feel and appearance of records, 78s and LPs alike. The blue/gold label of the Parlophone Rhythm-Style series, the magenta HMVs, the orange Vogues, yellow Esquires and black Brunswicks fascinated me. Later, the illustrated jackets of LPs provided further delights, particularly the splendid photographic sleeves of the late Fifties.

My heap of junked 78s included such diverse items as Michael Krein's "Saxophobia," Louis Armstrong's "Red Cap," Bing Crosby's "Please" and a mysterious, disturbing Duke Ellington gem called "Saddest Tale." I bore them away to my wind-up gramophone, played them incessantly and adored them all. Most of my pocket money was spent at Woolworth's before the war, where the cheaper record labels could be bought for ninepence. I was drawn to unusual names or song titles, so my very first purchases were by Brian Lawrence and his Landsdowne Sextet on Rex, and Teddy Powell's "Sans Culottes" on Regal. Some ten years later, I waited in a ferment of impatience for the initial issue of American Capitol 78's, having been intoxicated with the recordings of Stan Kenton, Nat King Cole, Peggy Lee, Nellie Lutcher and the like, broadcast during and after the war on the American Forces Network. A.F.N. programmes from Munich were easily picked up on radio and "Luncheon in Munchen," "Duffel Bag," "Midnight in Munich" and "The Vocal Touch" took precedence over the B.B.C.'s sparse offerings. The free-and-easy style of the Americans was welcome, too, and during the evening servicemen could phone in for a particular record or song and get it played almost immediately. When a certain disc was really popular, it was likely to receive several playings within two or three hours and I can never listen to Francis Craig's record of "Near You" without recalling the occasion when it would be played three or four times consecutively. One solder, infuriated by the repetition, sent a twenty-dollar bill to A.F.N. on the proviso that the disc jockey would break the record in half, while on the air. He did, but there were many other copies.

Towards the end of 1948, the Capitols appeared retailing at a hefty 5s. 9d. I was waiting outside Murdoch's record shop long before the 9 a.m. opening time and duly purchased Peggy Lee's "Manana," Pee Wee Hunt's "12th Street Rag," Nat King Cole's "Little Girl," Stan Kenton's "Artistry in Rhythm" and Nellie Lutcher's "Hurry On Down." Bliss. I had saved, scrupulously, to afford these luxuries and proceeded to blast my parents into submission with endless hours at the radiogram. The loud passages on the Kenton records played hell with my fibre needles, which needed constant sharpening in the IM Pointmaster. Fibres, which were purchased by the dozen in a container shaped like a top hat, could be bothersome as they were prone to snap or break down in mid-play but they didn't chew up the shellac like steel needles. Gradually, my taste veered away from my parents' more commercial preferences to the swinging big bands and, by 1947, to bebop, a form of modern jazz incomprehensible to the public at large. The frenetic up-tempo music of Charlie Parker, Dizzy Gillespie and the other boppers alienated the older generations, much as today's youth rebel against their parents, with music intelligible only to themselves. My mother and father hated jazz. "You'll grow out of it," they said.

That was almost forty years ago and rather than grow out of jazz, I have burrowed deeper into it as the years have passed. Much time and money have been spent in the record shops of Portsmouth. After the war, four or five shillings purchased a 78, but in 1952 the LP appeared, and it became necessary to produce up to 25s. for a 10-inch and 39s. 11d. for a 12-inch LP. My main source was again in Commercial Road – the Southsea branch, being a classical music bastion, only sold jazz records on sufferance and with some disdain. Presiding over the Commercial Road emporium like a malevolent gnome was Mr. White. Small bodied, large headed, gruff voiced, cynical and of indeterminate age, he eyed all schoolboys, as I was then, with deep suspicion and no amount of jocularity could extract even the bleakest smile from him. He was red faced, with hair centre-parted and a veined bulbous nose that would have done credit to W. C. Fields. His breath radiated stale booze, nicotine and other unknown horrors that were lethal from ten paces. No sooner were you ensconced in the tiny record booth with the latest Benny Goodman opus, than the door would burst open to reveal the narrowed eyes and pursed mouth from which emanated a blast of fetid air sufficient to render the cubicle noxious for several hours. "Don't scratch that LP, it's expensive!" he would snap. Or, after thirty seconds' listening: "Haven't you finished with that rubbish yet?" Sometimes, after lunch, by which time he'd downed more than a few jars, Mr. White would insist on putting on the records himself, "just to make sure." His hand, far from steady at best, frequently dragged the stylus across the pristine surface with disastrous results. "Indestructible, these LPs," he'd mutter thickly.

Towards the end of 1948, the Capitols appeared, retailing at a hefty 5s. 9d.

Papps, in North End, was a huge store stuffed full of pianos and other bulky instruments and was managed by an incredibly aged and short-sighted gentleman who was always tuning the Bechsteins and Steinways.

"I'd like that Dizzy Gillespie record in the window, please," I once asked him.

"Dicky who?" he wheezed. I knew I was in for trouble but it was one of those occasions when you just have to press on.

"Gillespie. Dizzy Gillespie." I smiled brightly.

"Izzy Valensky? Violinist, is he?" I assumed that all the piano tuning had done for his ears as well.

"No, Gillespie – Dizzy. JAZZ!"

"Chess? We don't sell . . ."

I was out of the door before I could heave a cello at him and didn't return until Jill, young, blonde and definitely hip, took over the record department. She used to give me a discount, too.

Wyatt's was a tiny shop in Queens Road, run by a pair of tall and vastly rotund brothers. They, too, regarded anyone under thirty who collected jazz with grave misgivings but they did possess an excellent stock of LPs and allowed you to disappear into a listening booth without undue interference. I began to spend rather a lot of money there and joined their Record Club, which allowed me to go into debt provided I made regular payments. As my account escalated, the Wyatts got into the habit of telephoning my parents to make sure that I hadn't left town. Then they sent me little reminder notices every few days and even stopped me in the street a couple of times to ascertain my future travel arrangements. I couldn't stand the pressure and decided to face the continual onslaught of Mr. White's dangerous digits and malodorous breath, instead.

More fascinating still were the second-hand or junk shops. The thrill of a discovery at a reasonable or even giveaway price motivates all collectors and neither the anticipation nor the excitement recedes with the years. Portsmouth must be the junk centre of the world. On the main road between North End and Fratton Bridge, along many of the roads that cross the route, or in Fawcett, Albert and Highland Roads in Southsea, second-hand shops of every description have risen overnight, like mushrooms, only to disappear in a few months to be replaced by a similar establishment. The cycle of opening and closing continues to this day as one shop load of rubbish settles briefly in the wake of another. Very often, buried deep in the mounds of sordid cast-off clothes, horrendous utility furniture and assorted garbage, would be a box of LPs or 78s. Most of them would be scratched beyond belief but now and again, some gloomy, chaotic, ill-lit, crumbling dump that reeked permanently of fried fish, cat's pee, or worse, would yield up a rare and precious gem in reasonable condition. It was worth all the dusty ferreting among the detritus, the dog hairs on your trousers, the dirt and grease on your jacket. You still had to find the proprietor, an assistant, anyone, to take the money, which was likely to be an unspecific amount yet to be haggled over. Whoever was holding the fort could be in the back room, upstairs in bed or down the road in a boozer or betting shop. It was a question of persistence and an overall desire to buy goods that the owner appeared reluctant to sell.

Fortunately, the specialist second-hand record shops were more permanent fixtures and certainly accepted your money with alacrity, though their hours of business could be arbitrary, few and irregular. Haskell and Green's in Lake Road was a lot of fun. The stock was large, turned over swiftly, always interesting and cheap but the real stars were H and G themselves. A dessicated double-act, they would emerge from a sordid doorway in the rear like Jimmy James and Eli staggering out from under a giant boulder. H (or G) would blink myopically behind his impenetrable lenses, spluttering "What is it, what is it?" through widely-spaced tombstone teeth. G (or H) stood in overcoat and cap, no matter the temperature or time of year. If approached for information or assistance he would shrug expressionlessly and say, " 'E'll know," nodding towards his partner or maybe, "Ask 'im." G's (or H's) principal function seemed to be the preparation of continuous supplies of tea and inch-thick jam sandwiches. Should he be left on his own for any reason he would refuse to take money for records or deal with anything a customer may require. Nodding towards the shop door he would force the words " 'E'll be back" through clenched lips or, perhaps, the less succinct " 'Ang on a bit."

There could be no greater contrast than Titmuss's in Arundel Street, where the lady of that name controlled the business with an iron hand and a beady eye. Standing tall, taller with her hair piled high, hands on hips behind the counter, she cast her laser beam on whoever might have the temerity to enter the premises. Even with your back towards her, you could feel the ray on the base of your neck as you riffled through the racks. It was unthinkable to leave without making a purchase and you were made to feel no more comfortable when parting with your money. "Cheap at the price. Amazing value!" she would rap out accusingly. You really felt that you should offer to pay double.

A short walk down the road brought you to "The House of Wax," run by that most dedicated of jazz enthusiasts, Frank Hurlock. He was a collector himself and there was always a fine selection of second-hand music and especially rare and numerous 78s in a Hurlock shop. A lot of good jazz conversation, too. Frank, who has been around all my life, was responsible for my introduction to the jazz intelligentsia, in 1947. A local advertisement drew me to a pub in Fratton where, in the upstairs room, the Portsmouth Jazz Club was about to hold its first meeting. I was in good time for the scheduled 8 p.m. start but a mere three or four half-cut people had staggered in by nine and it was shortly after 9.30 that Frank declared the meeting open. Our number had risen to a dozen when he played the first record, an Armstrong Hot Five. Bessie Smith, Jelly Roll Morton, Bechet, Ellington and Basie followed but, by 1947, I had been seduced by the modernists,

Parker, Gillespie, Navarro and Powell and it looked as if the P.J.C. was to cater only for "mouldy fygges."

Still, the club had to be patronised as there were few enough of us around and we should stick together, no matter how much we hated each other's favourite records. The second meeting brought only half-a-dozen swingers out into the raw December night and, as far as I know, there never was a third. But Frank was dauntless. His shops popped up and folded all over Portsmouth. Lake Road, Albert Road, Marmion Road and more. At this time, he's still dealing in 78s, ever the jazz fanatic and quite indestructible. Whenever I walk into his latest venture, he'll invariably greet me in that soft Pompey burr: "Hullo, mate. Still diggin' the sounds?" Yes, I am, thanks in some measure to the devotion and boundless energy of Frank Hurlock.

.....his breath radiated stale booze, nicotine and other unknown horrors.

CHAPTER ELEVEN

Cool Cats and Hot Nights

Live jazz was thin on the ground in the late Forties and early Fifties. Apart from the odd private club or someone's basement, there were very few premises where local amateur or semi-professional musicians might be allowed to blow unfettered. The Pomme D'Or club off Osborne Road was the meeting place. After it closed, the musicians – Arthur, Joe, Ken, Tony and a few others, mostly from the splendid semi-pro Johnny Lyne band – plus several enthusiasts, often drifted back to the flat over Stevens' butcher's shop at North End. Young Pete Stevens was a jazz buff, so the boys could play into the early hours without any aggravation. They played bebop and assumed the super-cool, laid back demeanour of their idols, whether performing or not. You could always pick them out. They would sit around in a tight little group, some in dark glasses, most with check overcoats, chewing gum and drinking coffee, black. Several heads would be nodding and feet patting in time to some bop anthem such as "Anthropology" or "Groovin' High", that they were hearing, communally, inside their skulls. They would speak infrequently and even then, briefly, though the occasional comment would elicit a chorus of manic laughs from the group. It would be a hip in-joke that they alone could understand.

It wasn't enough to dig the music; you had to blow to be accepted. You might approach them and speak to one or the other. A brief nod of recognition would be tantamount to a 21-gun salute but it was more likely that you would be completely ignored. Bravely, you could carry a chair across and join the group in a scatted version of "Night in Tunisia" or "Parker's Mood," which we all knew, note for note, even the non-musicians like Pip, myself, Dave and his sister April. Arthur kept up the bomb-dropping percussion accompaniment on a table top while Eddie, who carried his bongos everywhere in case he came across a gig where he could sit in, added the odd accentuation. At the finish, someone would breathe softly, "Yeaaah," and silence fell once more until a whispered aside from one of the elite sent the rest into paroxysms, falling about over their instrument cases. That's how it was with the boppers. They were real cool. Bloody rude, too.

Bill Cole was different. Blind from birth, he was a brilliant jazz pianist and always in unfailing good humour. You could meet Bill anywhere in Portsmouth, walking slowly but purposefully along the busy streets, knowing exactly where he was at all times. His ears were, as might be expected, incredibly sensitive and not merely at the piano. He could pick out a single voice in a crowd with the music blaring and he never forgot a name. I hadn't seen him for fifteen years and as I turned the corner from Kingston Road into Sultan Road, I bumped straight into him, sending him staggering back against the wall. "Sorry, Bill," I said, "didn't see you." "That's okay, Alan. You nearly knocked me over last time, too." A great Pompey character.

Most of our live music had to be paid for but there was always alternative entertainment if the sounds were disappointing. Friday nights were religious observances. First, the gang gathered at the Victory Bar, opposite the South Parade Pier. It would be bursting at the seams with sailors of every nationality, girls with dubious intentions and a few neglected locals. We would push our way through the raucous, randy masses and down a few rum and peps, the "in" drink, circa 1952. Having stacked up sufficient courage to brave a dance floor, we would sidle into the vast Savoy Ballroom next door. Friday night was Big Band night, when the resident musicians gave way to the famous orchestras of the day – Ted Heath and His Music, the Vic Lewis band, Oscar Rabin, Teddy Foster, the Squadronaires and many more. They all arrived in Southsea eventually.

Our modus operandi was simple but effective. From the balcony above the dancers we had a perfect view of the available talent. If a likely girl seemed to be unaccompanied, we would wait until the floor was crowded and then make our strike. It didn't matter if your footwork was lousy in a packed ballroom and it gave you an excuse to hold her closer while indulging in a little nuzzling. If your fancy was already with a partner, you had a decision to make. When approached, would he give way gracefully or get aggressive? If he got aggressive, could you cope with the subsequent attrition? There was always the possibility that the girl might tell you to get stuffed, whether she was accompanied or not, but you hadn't turned up to perfect your Fred Astaire routines. Bolstered by the rum and peps plus the additional top-ups from the Savoy bar, the rebuffs became acceptable and the ego remained relatively undamaged.

It was plain common sense never to take a girl with you on Friday nights. In the first place, you'd have to pay for her drinks at the Victory Bar plus her admission ticket for the

That's how it was with the boppers. They were real cool.

Savoy. In the second, there was the remote possibility that she might go off with someone else during the evening. A terrible loss, all round.

Most of the bands, famous and admired though they may have been, became strictly dancing, chatting-up or boozing background fodder on Fridays. One or two orchestras were special, however, and always merited your complete attention. Ted Heath's crew was crammed with great musicians like Jackie Armstrong, Tommy Whittle, Bobby Pratt, Kenny Baker and Jack Parnell. A crowd of several hundred would gather in front of the bandstand where you would be transported by the beautiful blast from eight brass and five saxes. When Lita Roza or Dickie Valentine sang, the lights in the hall were lowered and it was the perfect time to find your girl, stand close behind her with your arms around her waist and gently sway to the music. With the Vic Lewis band came euphoria. Britain's very own Stan Kenton boasted ten brass, my heroes being the saxists Ronnie Chamberlain and Kathleen Stobart, high-note trumpeter Harold Luff and cavorting, chortling trombonist Gordon Langhorn who later metamorphosed into Don Lang of Frantic Five infamy. The screaming Kenton favourites, "Painted Rhythm," "Peanut Vendor," "Intermission Riff" rang in your ears for hours.

Once in a while, a bop group would be the Friday attraction: Johnny Dankworth's Seven, Tito Burns' Sextet and even the Ronnie Scott Octet. As we arranged ourselves slap in front of the bandstand, the Scott group set off on a collection of pop numbers and left us cheated and disgusted. Boasting such fine jazz musicians as Jimmy Deuchar, Ken Wray, Derek Humble and Tony Crombie, it seemed an awful waste of talent. "How about some jazz, then!" I shouted at the end of a dire medley of current chart-topping drivel. Ronnie, obviously under orders from the management to keep the music danceable, had looked edgy from the start of the set.

"How much did you pay to come in?" he snapped crossly at me.

"Four shillings," I replied, "and it's not worth it."

Scott savagely thrust a hand into his pocket, paused, and drew it out again, empty.

"Pete," he said to altoist Peter King sitting next to him; "Pete, given him his bloody four bob."

King was not amused but found the coins and passed them across to me.

"Now piss off out of here," said Ronnie darkly.

I went home and on the following day sold all my Ronnie Scott records to a second-hand dealer. Charlie Parker wouldn't have carried on like that.

I was the only true jazz fanatic in the gang but a couple of old school friends were equally hooked on the stuff. Mike and I had both collected records with a savage rivalry since we first had enough money to buy a battered 78. We would spend hour after hour, taking turns at the radiogram, as first he would try to convert me to the joys of Sidney Bechet, then I would plead the cause of Fats Navarro. It was Armstrong versus Miles Davis, Artie Shaw versus Harry James, Muggsy Spanier against Howard McGhee until we both came round to enjoying each other's music. The rivalry then switched to finding new names, new talent. Mike would unearth Herbie Fields, I would discover Dodo Marmarosa. The same record would be played six, seven, eight times consecutively so that every note could be committed to memory. I found that the best way to ingest jazz was to jive about the room, head nodding, arms flapping. Mike invariably laid flat on the sofa, as if unconscious, and would only alter his position to fart – perhaps his greatest accomplishment. Like the famous French music hall artist, Le Petomaine, Mike could be relied upon to fart on demand and if he didn't possess his Gallic counterpart's ability to reproduce entire melodies, he nevertheless displayed a considerable versatility. Mike reckoned that the most fecund position for him to achieve the largest number and the greatest volume was to lie on his back, his legs pointing straight up in the air with his hands supporting the backs of his knees. He could then fire off a rapid machine-gun volley or a thunderous, sonorous salvo of three or four, as required. His piece-de-resistance was to hold a lighted match as close as safety allowed to the seat of his trousers

I was the only true jazz fanatic in the gang.

and, with any luck, the power and force of the ejected wind caused the flame to flare brightly and turn blue, simultaneously. Mike, thereby, set himself a standard he found difficult to surpass in later life.

My other long-standing mate was Pip. He was my only close Jewish friend and as placid as I was explosive. Pip was well-liked by everybody; youthful tantrums and enmities were not for him. He preferred his role as mediator, peacemaker, and perpetrator of dreadful puns, the only means by which he would ever be likely to annoy anyone. He was of medium height, slim and soft-spoken, his light blue eyes would cloud, appearing momentarily sightless and he would assume a vague, distracted air at moments of personal or communal stress. He was thus able to extract himself from the eye of the storm but possessed the ability to switch himself on again when the aggravation had subsided, as though absolutely nothing had happened.

I forgave Pip his verbal atrocities just as I overlooked his incapacity to shout and rave occasionally when the time seemed ripe. I even turned a blind eye to his inexplicable desire to become a soldier in the Guards and another blind eye to the sickeningly brilliant shine on his cadet corps boots. And on his ordinary shoes, as well! I ignored Pip's omnipresent neatness, creased trousers, tidy hair and relentlessly cheerful smile. In return, he overlooked all my excesses at all times and rendered me a great service into the bargain. It was he who introduced me to the contrapuntal joys of Dave Brubeck and Paul Desmond and he who knocked me for a loop with an American copy of a Sarah Vaughan LP with trumpeter Clifford Brown, an album that still gives me untold pleasure thirty years later. So does Pip's company, for our friendship endures to this day.

So it was with Mike, or Pip and a couple of the gang that I would go to South Parade Pier concerts on Sundays. There were two shows, at 2.30 and 7.30 and, again, we were offered a selection of the best big bands and small groups. The afternoon was for serious listening, so we sat in the stalls and copied out the list of numbers played for later discussion and evaluation. The evening show served an entirely different purpose. Upstairs, there was standing room behind the balcony seats and the gangway in which we stood not only faced the stage but circled around behind it. In other words, you could complete a 360-degree tour of the entire theatre. Every fifteen minutes or so we would stroll along the circuit looking for likely females and if you struck lucky, it was dark, quiet and deserted behind the stage. Even on a lean night, there was always the music. Pip has fond memories of the South Parade Pier. Watching a summer show there, he fell heavily for a sweet-faced chorus girl and summoning up immense reserves of courage, waited for her at the stage door. They went around together for quite a while – her name was Jill Gascoine.

CHAPTER TWELVE

In Labour

The unsavoury necessity of obtaining work became a persistent intrusion into my day-to-day existence. The unhappy times of wholesale unemployment were a long way in the future; in the Fifties, there were jobs in plenty for all comers. Although I had no obvious talents that fitted me for anything specific, my reasonable scholastic results and the fact that I had attended Portsmouth Grammar School resulted in the availability, however unfairly, of many and varied business opportunities. The trouble was, I couldn't take life or employment seriously, no doubt due to a severe dose of immaturity and a total lack of involvement with whatever I was supposed to be doing for a living. In the eleven years following National Service I had 32 jobs and not one of them gave me the slightest satisfaction or remotely engaged my interest.

Shamefacedly, I have to admit that it was all too easy. After scanning the Sits Vac columns of the local papers I would write, say, a dozen applications. On average, ten would reply with the offer of an interview and from there, I could usually talk myself on to the short list and even, directly into the job. That's when the problems began to mount for I would wilfully set about destroying my credibility, virtually daring employers to sack me by a combination of idleness, neglect and cheek until they either seized the nettle and did so, or I saved them the bother and resigned. The game of search, obtain and self-destruct dragged on until, at the age of thirty-two, I packed in the well paid post of area sales manager to become a professional songwriter. Then, for the first time in my life, it was a pleasure to wake up in the morning with the prospect ahead of an enjoyable day at work. Yet, despite my stupidity and perverseness, were those eleven years completely wasted? I think not, for I certainly learned a great deal about human nature and incidentally, about myself. Moreover, though much of that period had been a waste and a bore, I contrived to get involved in some ludicrous and hilarious situations, the memories of which remain priceless.

My first job was with a construction company that was building a housing estate at Horndean, a few miles outside Portsmouth. It was the hot summer of 1952 and I had somehow landed the position of assistant to the surveyor. I found myself on the telephone discussing "aggregate" and "hard core." Aggregate was something to do with the football league tables as far as I was concerned, and hard core . . . ? There was much lying about in the sun and the occasional game of cards with the labour force but eventually, Nemesis overtook me. By astute manipulation of a piece of equipment that he called a theodolite, my boss was laying out a new road. As he drove pegs into the ground marking the centre line, the heavy machinery came up behind and heaved all the earth away. Then the concreting lads moved in and another street was born. This highly technical description illustrates the extent of my understanding of the bewildering activity around me. I was aware that soon I would be expected to do something and my bluff would be called but it turned out much worse than that.

My employer dashed away on some emergency at another site and left me to complete the latest road. It was a piece of cake, he said. I had the plans, the theodolite, the lot, and in dire need I could always consult the foreman. Regrettably, I couldn't make sense of the plans, was unable to use the theodolite, and the foreman selected this precise moment to go sick. The following day was a Sunday, so I took a bus ride out to the estate where I would have the place to myself. I had a long look at the new road which had already been marked out for half of its length. It had begun to curve to the left slightly and I felt that it ought to continue on a gentle arc for fifty yards or so. Then, I thought, a straight bit at the end would look nice. I spent the rest of the day hammering in the pegs, ready for the men on Monday morning. Over the next 48 hours the transformation took place so that when the boss returned, my creation was completed. It displayed, I considered, an altogether attractive ambience. Unfortunately, a professional glance at the plans revealed that I had sent the road in the wrong direction, driving through a projected clutch of semi-detached houses. It was only Wednesday but they paid me for the full week. Probably a lot cheaper in the long run.

There followed a series of selling jobs lasting variously a few days or a few weeks but nearly all of them resulting in my being ejected from company or private premises with hardly a sale in the order book. Banging your head against a wall loses its charm eventually but I made one last bid for the Rep of the Year title by attending an interview at the resplendent Queens Hotel, in Southsea. An American organisation was looking for Advertising Space salesmen and after an initial chat with a crew-cut, Californian whizz-kid in a jazzy check jacket, I was shortlisted for the big one – a confrontation with the company psychiatrist.

The idea of matching wits with a genuine shrink rather appealed to me and I devised a witty line or two with which to make an impressive entrance. It didn't turn out that way at all for, responding to a sonorous call of "Come," I burst in radiating eagerness and energy only to find the room empty. I waited for a couple of minutes and was ready to forget the whole thing and go home when a black-suited, totally bald man wearing horn-rimmed spectacles appeared from under a table in a corner of the room. As I stood, gaping at him, he walked slowly towards me and raising his arms high, laid both hands on my shoulders saying: "I wish I had a son like you." Completely thrown, I stammered a few words of gratitude for the compliment. The dome in black held up a finger to his lips. "There's no need to thank me. I'm not your father." He spun round sharply, strode towards a large mahogany desk and perched on the corner, eyeing me suspiciously.

"What would you do if it rained strawberry jam?" he snapped, suddenly. Realising that this garbage was American for an intelligence test, I said the first words that came to mind:

"Go out and buy as many glass jars as I could afford." This sally produced a thoughtful nod.

"Who told you to say that?" He appeared rueful and a little taken aback.

"It just came to me," I answered truthfully, having obviously scored a direct hit with a gem of inspired improvisation.

"Have you spoken to any of the other applicants?" He was positively sullen now.

"No, I haven't." I was getting pretty annoyed myself.

"Steady, son," said my non-father. "We have to be very careful. A mistake at this stage could be disastrous."

I realised that I had already made mine by attending this charade but I could feel my anger dissolving fast and uncontrollable laughter looming large. It was time to get out of there.

"Is that all, then?" I inquired tersely.

"Who can tell," replied the eminent mind. "There is no beginning and no end."

"Oh yes, there is," I bellowed and rushed for the door. Outside in the corridor, I began to cackle hysterically. Had it really happened? Yes, it had. I failed the interview.

Shaken by this experience, I decided to opt for the safer confines of shop work. One of the multiple furniture combines in Commercial Road provided a haven for a couple of months. It was all a matter of seniority there. Mr. Nutley, the manager, had first pick of the customers; Stan, the senior salesman was next in line; Bill, who had strayed far south from his native Leeds was third and, as the new boy, I could have a crack at what was left. As commission formed a sizeable portion of our pay packets, it quickly registered that my earning capacity was severely limited. We all sat moodily behind a glass partition in a small office, eyes glued to the doors. It wasn't easy for Nutter, as he was inevitably called, to glue his eyes on anything for, behind his pebble specs, he was as blind as a bat. When the potential victims finally got within his focus, his lightning assessments were merciless. "Just friggin' about, them two," he'd mutter. Or: "Couldn't afford a bleedin' doormat." Also: "Keepin' out the soddin' rain, that's all."

Just occasionally, though, he would be galvanized by some mystical sixth sense, something quite beyond my comprehension that, for him, distinguished one very ordinary looking couple from the others. He would leap to his feet, myopic beads gleaming behind their magnifying glasses and swiftly run his hands through his Brylcreemed hair. "Stand back, lads", he'd say, rubbing his palms together furiously. " 'Ere goes a bedroom suite at least." Then he was away, false teeth clamped into a smile that was patently a confected leer, careering into the path of his prey. On went the posh accent: "Yes sir, yes madam, the perfect time to refurnish the 'ouse. We've just taken delivery of the very latest Scandinavian fitments." He would usher the couple to a pile of tat in the corner that had been hanging about since the war and dance attendance with a display of terpsichore and verbal ingenuity that would have done credit to Max Miller. You had to hand it to Nutter. He rarely let a fish off the hook and cheerfully loaded up the most poverty-stricken unfortunates with hundreds of pounds worth of furniture on HP that they clearly couldn't afford. "It'll all be back in a couple of months," he'd nod sagely, after the slaughter. "Hope they don't knock the shit out of it." His relentless destruction of the needy was imitated by Stan and Bill but I possessed neither the heart nor the nerve to follow suit with the few opportunities I was allowed. Nutter put me out of my misery eventually and handed me my cards. "Not your line of country, lad," he said. " 'Ave you considered dentistry or the law?" I promised to do so as soon as I got back from the Labour Exchange.

After a few more dead ends, I marched into Weston Hart's, the radio and TV shop in North End, and pleaded to see the managing director. He happened to buy suits from my father, so I was duly granted an audience on the spot. "Look," I explained urgently, "You've got a large place here, full of TVs with just a tiny corner given over to records. LPs are set to have a boom over here, so how about letting me build up your record department and make it the best in Portsmouth?" He shook his head firmly. "LPs will never catch on," he said with finality. "Far too expensive." He was unmovable and the reason I mention this is because, for once in my young life, I was dead right about something. Weston Hart's fell into line with other retailers, in due course, and stocked up with LPs but, by then, I had stumbled away to explore other blind alleys on my erratic journey.

An echo from the past provided an unwelcome diversion. As an ex-National Serviceman, I was committed to two weeks a year at a Territorial Army camp for the three years following demob. My first debacle was spent at Bude in Cornwall, where sleeping on duckboards in a well ventilated tent was no protection against the elements. For the second jaunt, to Towyn in Wales, I was at least re-united with Pip and another old schoolmate, Dave. In times when few of us could even drive, Dave possessed a luxurious Riley sports car, so we determined to drive to camp in style and, going for broke, concocted a ludicrous gesture of defiance. While the rest of the toy soldiers embarked on the train, we sped away on Dave's wheels and audaciously booked into the Corbett Arms Hotel, in Towyn. For ten days, we managed to wake early, drive the couple of miles to the camp, park the car under cover and creep within bounds, right on cue for the 6 a.m. parade.

On the eleventh morning, we were spotted entering camp and the game was over. As punishment, the three of us were placed on permanent cookhouse and latrine duty – a noble and hygienic combination – for the remaining four days and forbidden to leave the perimeter. After just 24 hours of this treatment and the tangible, if understandable, hostility of our compatriots, we thought we may as well go right over the top. Very late that night, Pip, Dave and I slid quietly out of camp and drove triumphantly back to Portsmouth, three days early. After the euphoria had evaporated, we waited for the wrath of the Territorial Army to descend upon us. Prison, three months in the real army, serving in the officers' mess – the horrific possibilities were endless. But nothing happened. Much later, I discovered a clue. The camp C.O. was a freemason, pushing hard for Worshipful Master, and my father held a senior position in the same Lodge. Could this explain the lack of retribution? Perish the thought.

Then I was back on the treadmill with more desultory jobs, including the Landport Drapery Bazaar, where I contrived to fall down a flight of steps holding a bale of material on the first afternoon. A plate glass window arrested my descent at some cost to its appearance and I beat a hasty retreat to a large chain store in Fareham. After three weeks of sweeping the floor and tidying the sweets counter, I was prompted by the paralysing boredom of it all to ask for a day off. It chanced to be the Jewish New Year and though a rampant atheist, I reckoned that I may as well get a little back for all the aggravation over the years. "Are you really Jewish?" enquired the manager, decidedly shaken by the revelation. Finally convinced of my awful secret, he called me into his office and handed me my cards. "I don't think you'll be suitable here," was his only explanation. Could it be, I wondered, that lacking a science degree rendered me insufficiently qualified to sweep floors? Legal letters flew back and forth between my parent's solicitor and the company and I eventually received £50 consolation for my 2000-year-old burden. There are a great many things that I shall never understand.

My antennae told me that it was time to make THE BIG EFFORT. I must get a job and keep it. W.H. Smith was to be the beneficiary of the new, serious, hard-working me and the regime duly commenced at its Albert Road branch, opposite the Kings Theatre. I tried, I really tried, but Mr. Strange the manager made it difficult. A short, dumpy man, whose hands only just peeped out of the sleeves of his omnipresent grey raincoat, he bore a strong resemblance to Peter Sellers as Dr. Strangelove. He spoke with his teeth clenched together, so that every utterance was delivered with a terrible smile and on a perpetual waft of his culinary favourite, garlic. He wasn't innately unpleasant but he was a nagger and a worrier. He actively enjoyed explaining everything ad nauseam, especially the obvious, always ending his perorations with "D'you see?" Thus, "The books should be stacked on the table like this, d'you see?" or "Envelopes pack away in the drawer this way, d'you see?" He would stand very close as he droned on, with the teeth and the breath, relief only arriving when a customer required attention or when it was the turn of some other member of staff to receive their facial. Then, he'd wheel away with a parting "D'you see?" and stump across the store, eager to deliver his next address. Strange didn't swing his arms when he moved but kept them rigidly at his sides, so taking on the appearance of a podgy toy soldier doing the slow march.

The rest of the shop staff was female, so the task of attending to the morning papers was mine alone. I would get up at 5 a.m., cycle the three miles to the shop, pick up the bundles of newspapers and magazines from the pavement outside and carry them through to a room at the back. There, I would sort out and address the papers and periodicals to be collected by the delivery boys at 6 o'clock. Frequently, if not late, one or two of them would fail to appear at all, leaving me to pedal around Southsea with a bulging carrier bag, trying to locate addresses on dark winter mornings.

The job done, I would ride home, wash, shave, have breakfast and get back to the shop. Strange was always there to note my time of arrival usually clicking his teeth in disapproval while burrowing for his watch on a wrist swathed in layers of shirt, pullover, jacket and raincoat. "Tch, tch, after nine again, d'you see?" I saw, Christ how I saw. I found it increasingly difficult to keep my temper. He was there all the time and when we weren't eyeball to eyeball, the rancid breath drifted across from behind my back.

"It's all a matter of application and method, d'you see?"

"A bottle of ink can look really attractive, properly presented in the right surroundings, d'you see?"

I developed shingles from the accumulated aggravation and after the first couple of days at home, Strange becan to call regularly, every morning, to check on my recovery. "The work's piling up, d'you see?" What really griped him was having to do the papers each day, particularly as one of the boys had left, giving him the pleasure of a dawn patrol along Southsea sea front in the depths of winter. I dragged my ailing body back to Smith's but things were no better. The crunch came at stocktaking time. Each evening after closing and all week-end, we counted everything in the place. Not merely books but birthday cards, pens, pencils, drawing pins, paper clips, rubber bands – every minute, irritating, trivial object had to be accounted for. Strange was everywhere, supervising, checking, re-checking, stumping around the shop in a lather of sweat and garlic, for fear that some infinitesimal error might reflect unfavourably upon his efficiency. He drove us all berserk and I was very close to chucking in the whole rotten business. The old me would have long since done so.

It was a quiet Wednesday morning, half-day closing, so we started stocktaking before we closed at 1 o'clock. Strange continued his manic harassment of the staff. It started to rain and a table full of Neville Shute books, placed as a special display in the forecourt of

"What would you do if it rained strawberry jam?"

the store, was in danger of getting damp. The manager detailed me to help him move the table. We stood either side of the display and he gave the command, "Lift." I lifted my side slightly more than his and a book fell on to the rain-soaked forecourt. "You fool, you fool," he screamed. He pounced on the book, picked it up and wiped it back and forth on my sleeve. "Look at it, look at it! It'll have to be remaindered now, d'you see? You're useless, useless. You can't do anything!" He banged me once more on my arm and that was it. I couldn't take the nagging, the teeth, the breath a moment longer. I swung a left uppercut into the jaw immediately before me and was amazed to see Strange take off, upwards and backwards, to land right in the middle of the display table. Books flew everywhere as he toppled on to the ground and stared up at me in disbelief, for once speechless. One of the Neville Shute's had slid out across the pavement and was quite soiled and sodden. Strange scrambled over to pick it up. It was "In the Wet."

I waited for the inevitable bullet. There seemed little point giving in my notice as I would only lose six weeks' dole money. Strange wasn't hurt but, given the circumstances, that was surely irrelevant. The outcome astonished us all for, instead of being fired, I was transferred to Smith's newer, larger, modern branch in Palmerston Road, the classiest part of Southsea.

Now a new danger lurked because, here, the manager was a Victorian martinet. Mr. Pritchard was thin, tall and straight-backed. Though probably no more than thirty-five, he was very bald and his prissy Hitlerian moustache above pinched, thin lips combined with steely eyes behind rimless spectacles to give him an appropriate appearance of the utmost severity. Indeed, placed inside an SS uniform he would have been a ringer for Heinrich Himmler. A cold, hard, unsmiling man, he spoke with quiet menace in a high, unmodulated voice so that each commonplace utterance assumed the dimensions of a serious threat. The invariable dark suit, white wing collar, dark blue shirt and plain grey tie accentuated the ensemble effect. I always felt that he was about to plunge a hypodermic needle into my arm and say: "In a few seconds, you will tell me everything."

Our relationship began quite agreeably. Pritchard made no mention of my Albert Road shenannigans and soon dispatched me on a short training course at the firm's Kingston, Surrey, branch. This little venture was highlighted by a brief, intensely passionate affair with the girl behind the stationery counter who apparently left to join the W.R.N.S. as soon as I returned to Southsea. What did I say? Back at Palmerston Road, the war of nerves got under way. Whereas one was always aware of Strange's presence, Pritchard was sneaky. He hid in the alcoves, behind book displays and around corners. He was forever watching, watching. And after the watching, came the lecture. You were called into his office and stood to attention while he quietly tore you apart. Every minuscule defect and personal inadequacy was dissected. Your shoes were in need of polish, socks too bright, fingernails filthy, shirtcuffs frayed, suit unpressed, hair unkempt, tie askew. Your manner was insufficiently deferential, service sluggish, knowledge sketchy and delivered ungrammatically. Dotheboys Hall was alive and well. I stuck it for some months but could feel the red mist building up and gave in my notice before I was forced to give Pritchard a dose of the Neville Shutes.

Quo Vadis, I asked myself. It seemed that every avenue in Portsmouth had been exploited, every possibility exhausted. Here I was, twenty-three, unemployed again and directionless. Maybe it was time to explore the lusher pastures of the capital, where I was mercifully unknown. An old army friend offered to share his digs with me, so I took off to Hendon and set about the Sits Vac columns in the London "Evening Standard." It was the same old routine. Selling jobs came and went. The Imperial Tobacco Company sacked me because I didn't smoke, a radio and TV shop in Brewer Street sent me packing when I refused to stand out on the pavement and "shlep in" the customers as they walked past.

My brief association with the Handy Angle Company certainly qualified for entry in my catalogue of bizarre experiences. A handy angle was a piece of metal with slots, like a piece of Meccano, bent into an "L" shape for securing and joining rows of shelving in storerooms and factories. The company was another of those transatlantically motivated organisations that didn't allow you to sell using your own personality and ability. They had prepared a typewritten, foolscap screed which was to be memorised and delivered exactly, down to the last exclamation mark. You were to speak the words on the page precisely as written and in the correct order. No provision was made for the fact that you might receive a verbal response which made immediate nonsense of your next pre-prepared remark. If your customer asked you the time or wanted a light for his cigarette, you were sunk.

Once you had gained admission to the buyer's office, you walked towards him with your right hand behind your back holding a handy angle. As the buyer said "How do you do?" and held out his hand to shake yours, you smartly whipped your hand from behind your back and slapped the handy angle into his palm, saying simultaneously: "How do you do? I'm handy angle." Being rather more civilised in those innocent days, the assumption was that whoever you met would automatically shake your hand in greeting, even if his next move was to throw you out.

With the handy angle duly presented, you were off and into your spiel. The next line was: "Have you ever seen anything like this before?" This struck me as pure folly, offering carte blanche to a sadistic buyer with an original turn of phrase. As it turned out, I didn't get past my opening gambit. I managed the "How do you do? I'm handy angle" bit with great nonchalance but as I whipped up my hand holding the angle, I miscalculated slightly and ripped a generous portion of skin off my client's knuckles. Blood poured on to the carpet and the balance of my oration remained undelivered. I left both the premises and the company's employ before I could be charged with assault.

My last fling in the wicked city was with Lyons. I presented myself at the famous Corner House in Coventry Street, bent on making a good impression. Bathed, shaved and in my best suit, I hoped that I epitomized what the firm had advertised for – a trainee restaurant manager. I was totally unprepared, however, for what transpired. Fully expecting to swan about the Salad Bowl, enjoying the music, nodding to the customers, flirting with the waitresses and ushering people to their tables, I was instantly bundled into a lift which sank without trace, deep into the bowels of the earth. When it finally stopped, I stepped out into what appeared to be a vast dungeon, the only light emanating from a small office in the far corner.

A tiny man in a bloodstained white apron stood in the doorway, beckoning me with his little finger.

"You got the ducats?" he enquired in a strange mittel-Eurpoean accent, as I approached.

"Have I got what?" I asked. He raised his eyes ceilingwards in a gesture of impatience.

"The ducats, you got the ducats?"

I tried to explain that far from being a numismatist, I was waiting to be trained for an important executive position in the company. The gnome nodded and poked inside his ear with a matchstick.

"Ja, Ja," he said, "but did you bring the ducats?"

Before I could place my hands around his neck, a smart grey-costumed woman loomed out of the darkness. "Here you are, Heine," she said to the bloodied manikin. "Here's the dockets you wanted." The DOCKETS! I made a mental note to try and come to terms with the London accent at my earliest opportunity.

I outlined my circumstances to the lady. She listened attentively, said "Won't keep you a moment," and disappeared into the stygian gloom. Heine wandered off to some blood-soaked Lilliput where ducats rule and, very soon, the only sound was a distant tapping, as if something in the crepuscular interior was trying to pass me a warning message. Some ten minutes elapsed and a young lad in a long white coat materialised, handed me a large piece of white cardboard, and left. Joe Lyons certainly had a keen sense of theatre, even if the dialogue left something to be desired. I looked at the white card which had a pig drawn on it. The animal was divided into sections by dotted lines but there was no explanation as to what each section represented. A further five minutes drifted by and then a trundling sound preceded another white coat pulling along a dead pig on wheels. The sorry mess stopped in front of me and the white coat handed me a box containing several terrifying knives.

"What's this for?" I asked nervously.

"You've got yer card, aintcher?" inquired the coat. I nodded. "Well, thems yer cuts and thems" – indicating the knives – "thems yer knives." The coat grinned evilly and departed.

Me? Cut up a dead animal? In my best suit? In any suit! I stabbed the carcass in the side with one of the knives and leaving the haft juddering in that twilit hades, located the lift and returned to the living world.

CHAPTER THIRTEEN

The Odd Couple

Portsmouth was very much as I'd left it. At least, my mother was pleased to have me back, though I truly wondered why. I had never given her anything to boast about. To be precise, I'd been nothing but trouble since being pregnant with me caused her to put on far too much weight and lose her teeth. In her teens and twenties she was very beautiful and remained a handsome woman all her life, which was a constant battle with calories. Her weight see-sawed violently as each crash diet was succeeded by another bout of picking. Mum never ate large amounts – she picked. Before and after meals, morning, afternoon and evening, she would nibble a biscuit here, a piece of cake there. She never stayed in one place long enough to consume a reasonable lunch or a sizeable dinner for she spent the entire day on the move. She ran to the kitchen, to the shops, to the living room and when, in later life, she was manageress of a shop, she ran around that, too.

And my mother worried. About everything and everybody. Generous to a fault with love, time and money, everyone's problems were hers and if she ever had a moment's peace, I managed to shatter it with my demanding selfishness and lack of consideration. It had always been difficult for her. My paternal grandmother was the archetypal Jewish monster. A woman of vast size, she dominated and controlled the lives of her husband, daughter and four sons, of whom my father was the eldest. While she lived, none of them made a move without her consent and each was in thrall to her every whim.

Though my mother was never considered to be "good enough" by my grandmother, to his credit, my father hung on grimly through a seven-year engagement and finally succeeded in marrying her. He was by no means out of the wood. The tentacles maintained their grip, the dear octopus had first claim on his time and company and he didn't have the will to resist. The saloon car would draw up outside and whisk my father off to his parents' house, leaving his wife and brat at home. What with his masonic nights and his snooker nights, too, life was far from perfect for my mother. She was granted an audience, however, on Friday evenings when the entire family congregated for dinner. Then, my grandmother would crush me to her enormous bosom, call me "bubbala" and cover me with kisses and compliments, while shoving chocolates into any available orifice. There were boxes of confectionery everywhere throughout the house; the place was a shrine to Terry's and Cadbury's, so I was prepared to suffer the smotherings and gushings in return for the coffee creams.

Grandmother's death, in 1942, wrought an amazing metamorphosis, my father's dependence upon her being instantly transferred to my mother. From being scarcely considered, she was made responsible thereafter for major decisions regarding the home, business, finances, and me. While he would play football or cricket with me, my father could never cope with my education, discipline and the myriad problems that beset a

My mother remained loving and fiercely loyal through all my excesses. . . . . my father, a master craftsman who never tired of his work.

small boy. "Ask your mother" became the standard reply to practically everything. Somehow, she managed both of us but it was hardly surprising that the only son was prodigiously spoilt and reacted accordingly, with constant demands for further indulgences.

My mother remained loving and fiercely loyal through all my excesses, the bad behaviour at home, the idleness at school, the trying two years of National Service, the bewildering and unsatisfactory succession of jobs and the numerous girl friends. Care deeply as she did, Mum was desperately concerned not to behave like a possessive Jewish mother. She made the occasional scene when to remain silent would have caused her to burst but generally she allowed me free and generous rein. Except with girls. "I'm a feminist," she announced from time to time, long before the cry became commonplace. "In any argument between male and female, I always side with the woman," she would say. And so she did, frequently taking the part of any girl to whom she considered I was being less than fair. My mother's straight back and bearing gave her the appearance of a much taller woman and when roused from her natural reticence, she made a formidable opponent. Certainly, I never won a battle with her when she was determined to have her way, and my father didn't even bother to try.

Dad must have been the most naive man in the world, sheltered from life's major problems and decisions by two women until he was past seventy. He thereby coasted along apparently unaffected by the slings and arrows, immune and oblivious to trauma and upheaval. Perhaps not surprisingly, he remained unfailingly good-humoured, chipper and jovial. A mere five feet two inches tall, though he insisted that he was really five feet four, my father went bald at an early age, a loss that bothered him greatly. He swore that a defective piece of carbolic soap had caused the fall-out and told me countless times that "If I knew then what I know today, I'd still have a healthy head of hair." No amount of medical proof or reasoned argument would shake his belief, not even the fact that his two brothers, who resembled him closely, had also lost their hair. He went to extraordinary lengths to induce his scalp to produce a fresh growth, trying every lunatic cure, lotion and substance that came to his attention. Back in the late Twenties, he even underwent electrical treatment and bought a crazy contraption that I would dearly have loved to witness in operation. Having wired himself up and fixed the complicated apparatus, he would place a metal cap over his head, secure it under his chin with straps and switch on the current. There he'd sit for an hour or so, twice a day, while the electrical impulses sent the metal hat bumping up and down on his scalp, producing the friction that was supposed to encourage a new crop of hair.

Born in 1900, my father went straight from school into the family tailoring business, only retiring at the age of seventy-six. He was the cutter and front man in the shop and a great many of the customers were his masonic brethren. He was also a master craftsman who never tired of his work over 64 years and during that lengthy period never took a day off nor suffered an illness of any kind. As he grew older, he loved to think of himself as the oracle dispensing the accumulated wisdom of his years to less fortunate mortals. When he was out of his depth in any particular discussion, he would ask for your opinion and, while you delivered your thesis, would stand there nodding sagely, murmuring "Of course, of course," as though he were simply checking that you were as well informed on the subject as he was. Dad would never admit to ignorance of anything. I once found him watching Open University on TV – the subject was "Thermodynamics in Action" – and he sat there nodding away in agreement, muttering "Of course, of course." On another occasion, I took him along to a barbecue given by some American friends. He was drawn

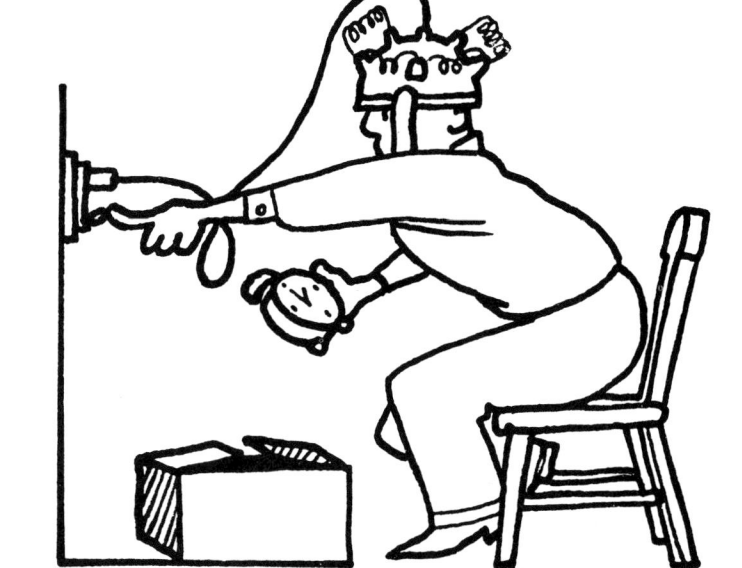

Having wired himself up......he would switch on the current.

to a heated discussion by several university professors who were vehemently denouncing Nixon for his blatantly culpable involvement in the Watergate scandal. My father stood at the edge of the group, nodding importantly as the Americans decimated their president, clearly without the vaguest notion of what they were talking about. There was a sudden pause in the conversation and Dad seized his chance to join the faculty. "Tell me," he said, glancing around his captive audience. "That chap Nixon. Do you think he had anything to do with this Watergate business?"

Dad found it expedient to agree with everybody at all times and it obviously paid off because I am unaware that he had an enemy in the world. He had his likes and dislikes, though, and rated himself as quite a music buff. "I'm a highbrow, you know," he once told me, going on to praise Julie Andrews, Elaine Paige and Nat King Cole, and applying his ultimate criterion: "You can hear every word." To be fair, he did enjoy Beethoven ("what grandeur"), Bach ("should be pronounced correctly. Can't stand BARK") and the violinist Isaac Stern ("he's Jewish, you know."). My father was equally opinioned in films, being convinced that foreign movies were "a lot of bullshit," consisting only of "tits and arses." He, nevertheless, contrived to watch them at every opportunity on TV and would roll about with laughter during the love scenes. "They're having a good feed," he'd chortle. As with foreign films, so with foreign food, all of which he denounced as "muck." Once, out shopping, he picked up an aubergine and asked my wife what it was. She told him. "Ugh," he said, dropping the fruit as if it were venomous. "Putrid!" Foreigners, too, came under the lash, Germans, Arabs and Argentines being collectly

The London Road, North End, shop c. 1930. My father, with his youngest brother, scouting for business.

dismissed as "bastards." Slightly less offensive were trades union leaders, vandals and homosexuals – "bleeders," all.

Until my mother had a stroke in 1972, Dad had never made a cup of tea, a piece of toast, or boiled an egg. Though severely incapicatated, Mum managed to teach him sufficient basic cookery and programmed him to do the cleaning, washing and general running of the home. Although seventy-two, he cared for her until she died, and was able to look after himself with complete success until he was past eighty. It was a considerable achievement and I came to appreciate his qualities much more in his final years. Oliver Goldsmith was once described as "a good natured man with no harm in him" and this definition suits my father well. He was quite unsullied by the evils around him, forgave those who sinned against him, being willing even to befriend them and retained a childlike innocence to the end. At the age of seventy-five, he asked me: "Tell me, Al boy, what is a French letter?" Knowing my father as I did, I'd often wondered how I ever made it into the world. When he asked me a question like that, however, I think I may have stumbled across a logical explanation.

CHAPTER FOURTEEN
Rose Rheum

My parents led a quiet, sober life, which is probably why they grew very fond of the gang's noisy omnipresence in their home. Gradually, they became ensnared in the lives of them all, dispensing affectionate interest and solid or liquid refreshment in generous proportions. My mother lent a sympathetic ear to personal problems and predicaments while proffering the loaded tray and Dad used us all as subjects to supplement his growing preoccupation with photography.

Though doubtless preferring to turn his lens exclusively on to the ever-changing parade of girlfriends whom we introduced to his lounge, my father's chef d'ouvre was his magnificent series of 1952-53 photographs – crazy poses, trick shots, tableaux and set pieces – which I fortunately preserved in albums. Superbly clicked off on his Zeiss Ikon, developed and printed himself, these photos have been dragged out of the cupboard countless times over the years, never failing to send my father into hysterics. "Great days, great days," he always chuckled.

Not content with the prospect of toppling Henry Cartier Bresson from his pinnacle, Dad was then seized with an inexplicable desire to grow roses. The centre-piece of our sizeable lawn had been a magnificent growth of pampas grass but my father demolished the lot, replacing it with a circular bed of small rose bushes, in the centre of which stood his pride and joy, an expensive, sturdy, burgeoning standard rose. He lavished time and love on this splendid growth while conducting a vicious war against any insect foolish enough to stray into the garden.

The lawn had always been the gang's private football and cricket pitch. Dad accepted the wear and tear on the grass philosophically, though principally, I suspect, because he fancied himself as goalkeeper and wicketkeeper. With the advent of the roses, however, he grew edgy and fearful for their safety, declaring the garden to be a future non-playing area. Thenceforth, we restricted our games to the hours when my father was at work, cunningly covering the balding goal areas with freshly mown grass cuttings. All went well until one of my wickedly curling free-kicks cannoned into the revered standard rose, snapping it neatly in half. Roger's maniacal laughter and Bud's goofy grin faded swiftly as we began to appreciate the likely repercussions of this cruel blow. No more football, cricket or photos, no more coffee, cake and biscuits; worst of all, no use of the lounge with its attendant bonuses.

I looked at the pathetic, shattered rose stump, tethered with tape to its supporting bamboo stake, and had a great idea. Picking up the sundered top section, I placed it neatly on top of the lower half, holding it steady while Will welded the two pieces together with generous lengths of tape, finally strapping the "repaired" trunk to the

He bought every available insect repellent, compost and fertilizer.........

bamboo pole support. It looked terrific. Nemesis, we realised, was on its inevitable way but, at least, we had delayed its arrival.

During subsequent days, the standard rose languished. Its leaves yellowed and withered and it gave every indication of being terminally sick. My father was shattered. He bought every available insect repellent, compost and fertiliser, mulched tea leaves into the soil, sought the advice of gardening experts. After a sharp, evening rain shower he would creep down the garden with a torch to see if some life-blood had been drawn into the invalid's veins. He stood at his bedroom window, opera glasses trained on the rose bed, hoping to head off a marauding cat that might be peeing and spraying his tree into oblivion. He joined the library, staggering home under a pile of gardening books, one of which suggested that talking to plants was a positive method of inducing growth.

Accordingly, Dad would nip home at lunchtimes and lavish endearments and blandishments upon the stricken object. Exasperated by the lack of tangible improvement, he eventually resorted to shouts and threats, the garden reverberating to his regular cry of "Grow, you bugger, grow!" He seemed to be forever by the rosebed, shaking his head sadly and mumbling: "I can't understand it. I just can't understand it."

The measure of my father's desperation may be gauged by the fact that, one evening, he arrived home with one of his old Home Guard cronies from Denmead. God knows why, but Dad had somehow come to the conclusion that the permanently drunk Wally was a gardening expert. Wally lurched dangerously towards the roses and peered myopically at the shrivelled tree. He was obviously three and a half sheets to the wind already.

"What is it?" he muttered irritably, swaying gently.
"What is it?" echoed Dad. "It's a bloody rose tree."
"Bollocks," rumbled Wally. "It's one o' they continental jobs – Japanese, I s'spect."
My father looked a broken man. This had not been one of his better decisions.
"Yeah. That's it," spluttered Wally, thickly. " 'Er don't like our weather, y'see."
Dad's eyes rolled heavenwards. When would this nightmare end?
"Too cold. I say it's too cold over 'ere." Wally was getting into his stride now.

My father tugged at the wise old countryman's sleeve, endeavouring to remove him from the scene. Wally stumbled heavily, simultaneously trampling a rose bush to extinction with his left boot while snagging his right trouser leg on the thorns of another. He pulled hard, ripping off a branch and several blooms.

"Tough little buggers, ain't they," he grinned, farting loudly.

Dad helped him across the grass towards the house. Wally stopped, leaned heavily on my father's shoulder and looked back at the standard rose. He winked knowingly.

"Pull 'er up and re-pot 'er in the greenhouse, that's my advice. She'll 'ave berries all over 'er next year."

As a final forlorn gesture, Dad bought a length of electric cable and rigged up a spotlight beside the sad plant. Perhaps the light, the warmth, some form of transference might effect a miracle. In the event, Mother Nature entered from on high and brought an end to the fruitless vigil. It rained remorselssly for several days and the gales blew mightily, a combination that caused the tape holding up the rose to gradually loosen, unwind and fall away.

One morning, my father found the top section of his standard rose lying on the earth, revealing the splintered truth. But the explosion I had expected never materialised. The effort he had expended and the length of time that had elapsed since the initial trauma had obviously drained his emotions. He was now simply exhausted by the entire episode and somehow relieved to discover that he was in no way to blame for the tree's demise. That knowledge seemed to satisfy him and his quiet acceptance of my belated admission of guilt affected me more than if he had gone berserk with rage.

Dad lost all interest in rose growing from that moment, so the football and cricket matches resumed in due course. To his credit, my father came to appreciate the humorous aspects of the affair and, indeed, gained some sort of recompense by dining out on the saga of the standard rose at numerous functions until the end of his life, 30 years later.

CHAPTER FIFTEEN

On the Floor

So there I was back where I started from, in Portsmouth, out of work and fast running out of options. One of the few major retailers yet to avail themselves of my services was Marks and Spencer, by far the most desirable in terms of career prospects, and certainly the most difficult to infiltrate. With little hope, I attended a preliminary interview and, surprisingly, was selected to go forward to a second, more searching examination. Incredibly, I passed this, too, and was shortlisted for a final thorough interrogation. To my own and my parent's disbelief, I was accepted into the company as a trainee departmental manager and it seemed that I had cracked it, at long last. With the interviews being spaced over several months and but negligible hope of a successful conclusion, it was necessary to find other employment, meanwhile. I went back on the treadmill with a few more dismal forays into the world of commerce.

After one or two typical howlers, I commenced, with great reluctance, a job at another multiple furniture store located but a few yards from the scene of my past debacle with Mr. Nutley. To my dismay, I was sent to the carpet department and placed in the charge of Abe Schenk. Schenk was a living caricature of a London East End Jew – indeed, he came from Aldgate – and possessed all the mannerisms that, perhaps I should be ashamed to say, I find hysterically funny. Very small, very bald, overweight, he had the busy waving hands, self-deprecating tilt of the head, the glottal, nasal London Jewish accent complete with the over-accentuated "T" and incompletely pronounced "R." Peter Ustinov and Peter Sellers have perfected the voice a thousand times on radio and film. He was surprised to see me in the shop: "Your family got a business and you ain't in it?" The head was on one side, the hands spread, eyebrow arched in mock amazement. I assured him that I was intent on making a million under my own steam. "Schmuck," he said, with an expressive shrug of the shoulders that effectively consigned me to a padded cell.

Schenk left me alone for a few days though I sensed him watching me, surreptitiously, but after the first week had passed and I still hadn't made my first sale, he called me into his office. He motioned me to sit down with a contemptuous wave of his arm.

"You a Yiddisher boy and you can't sell?" It was more an accusation than a question.

"I just can't get involved with the product," I said.

"Involved? Involved? What's to get involved? If you can sell, you can sell."

The logic was irrefutable but the fact was that I hated carpets, the store and everything in it. I sat there, looking pitiful.

"Listen, listen," said Abe, dropping a heavy hand on to my shoulder. "Selling's like a love affair, already. You can yence can't you? You've chavered a shikse, haven't you?" I nodded, smiling lecherously. "Well, selling's making love. You make love to the

"Your family got a business and you ain't in it?"

customer and you're in love with the shmutter you're flogging her. It's eye contact, eye contact. You make her want you and when she wants you, she wants the carpet. You understand what I mean?"

I looked at Abe Schenk, the large nose set in the perspiring face, the hairless head, the pot belly, and tried to imagine a customer wanting him. But later that day, I could see what he meant. He fluttered around a captive housewife like Nureyev. His footwork was masterly, the undulating hands and gyrating body complementing the twinkling toes to perfection. Sweating wildly, he peered closely into the woman's eyes. "You can trust me," the little brown beads seemed to be saying. "Such a carpet," he sighed, "so exactly right for the house beautiful." He stroked the multi-coloured horror on the floor as if he were about to propose marriage to it. "See the pile? Lavish! Lavish!" The lady was truly mesmerised by the dance, the verbal flow, the hypnotic eyes, the lot. Another deal was clinched, money exchanged.

Afterwards, Abe sat in his office, mopping his face. "See what I mean, lobbas? It's a love affair, a love affair." I expressed my admiration for his performance and also my doubts concerning my own ability. "Spunk. That's what you need, boy. Spunk." I wandered away, not wanting to get involved in this particular development in the conversation. A little later, I failed miserably to induce a customer to purchase a modestly priced fireside rug. As she walked away, I could hear Abe in his office, grumbling audibly: "No spunk. He's got no spunk." I wished he wouldn't keep on using that word. The second week came to a close and I still hadn't clinched a sale. Along with my pay packet, I was handed my cards together with a printed note, hoping that I would have a successful future in more suitable employment. It was fair enough. I said goodbye to Abe, who stood by his office door, shaking his head sadly.

"And you a Yiddisher boy," he grimaced, wagging his head continually. "You know your trouble, don't you?"

"Yes, Mr. Schenk," I said solemnly. "No spunk."

Practically everybody holds Marks and Spencer in great esteem, and rightly so. The company's standards are of the highest, the merchandise is excellent, the staff are well paid, well treated and there's a profitable future for the diligent and ambitious employee. My preliminary stints in the stockroom and the administration offices were agreeable and enjoyable. I progressed to the shop floor and from then on, every moment was purgatory.

I found it impossible to get deeply involved in the respective sales of grey and brown socks, to be wildly enthused about the correct positioning in the appropriate counter of lovat green trousers, or to have a passionate interest in the potential of Angel Cake as opposed to Dundee Cake. It requires a special kind of person to get excited about bras and panties when there's nothing inside them. I did try. For fifteen months, I strode around the store simulating concern, eager and businesslike, my check lists always in my hand, pen poised to make entries and comments that would revolutionise sales marketing. But I was bored, bored. I knew it was the last chance saloon, that my parents would be heartbroken if I threw away this great opportunity to secure a lucrative career with an admirable organisation. But it was my life – and I was hating it.

With my twenty-fifth birthday approaching, I resolved to make that day the watershed. I still hadn't discovered what I was any good for and my pastimes devoured my energies and commitment. But, surely, I must be good for something? Whatever it was, it wasn't Marks and Spencer. Sooner or later they'd see through my affected enthusiasm; they probably had, already, and I couldn't keep up the pretence indefinitely. I was 25 on Tuesday, May 15, 1956, and on the following Saturday I handed in my notice.

With my popularity at home reaching an all-time low, it made good sense to give London another chance. Portsmouth, no doubt, would be grateful for the respite. In any case, the gang was spread far and wide by now, each member chasing his own destiny. Of course, I wasn't to know and certainly wouldn't have believed that the years ahead would provide even more ludicrous surprises than those I had hitherto survived. Indeed, the next twenty-five years made the first quarter of a century look pretty tame. And that, if you can bear it, could be another story.